ZACK C. WOOTEN

The Azores Travel Guide 2025

An Ultimate Handbook for Exploring Portugal's Enchanting Islands.

Contents

Disclaimer

This book is designed to be your trusted companion for exploring your chosen destination. It provides in-depth insights and practical advice to help you make the most of your trip. While every effort has been made to ensure the accuracy of the information at the time of writing, travel conditions and local details can evolve.

Please note that this guide does not include images or maps. Instead, it focuses on delivering rich content to prepare you for an unforgettable experience.

Trust this guide to give you the foundation, and let your adventure fill in the rest.

Welcome to the Azores

Discovering the Azores

The Azores, an archipelago of nine volcanic islands in the heart of the Atlantic Ocean, stand as one of the world's prime examples of nature's artistry. Situated about 1,500 kilometers west of mainland Portugal, these islands attract travelers with their blend of scenic landscapes, rich history, and vibrant local culture.

The Allure of the Azores

Each island of the Azores boasts a unique charm that makes the archipelago a must-visit destination. From the misty forests and ancient volcanic craters of São Miguel to the vineyards draping over the lava stone walls in Pico, the diversity of the landscapes invites exploration and admiration. The islands offer a relatively mild climate year-round, with temperatures rarely dropping below 14°C in winter or rising above 25°C in summer, making them an ideal destination for those seeking a temperate escape.

Geography and Natural Beauty

The Azores are famed for their dramatic landscapes, which include lush greenery, towering cliffs, and serene lakes curled up in volcanic craters. São Miguel, the largest island, is home to the Sete Cidades Lake, a twin-lake situated in a massive caldera. Here, visitors can take in the stunning view where one side of the lake reflects a deep blue and the other a vivid green due to its vegetation. Pico Island, named after its imposing mountain, offers challenging hikes that reward climbers with breathtaking views across the archipelago and, on clear days, to the neighboring island of Faial.

The islands are a hotspot for geothermal activity, which can be seen in the fumaroles and hot springs scattered across them, particularly in Furnas on São Miguel. Here, travelers can experience the therapeutic properties of the mineral-rich waters or taste the unique local cuisine cooked underground by the natural heat.

Cultural Tapestry

The Azores have a rich maritime history that dates back to their discovery in the 15th century by Portuguese navigators. The cultural impact of centuries of maritime activity is evident in the local architecture, with charming Portuguese colonial buildings lining the coasts and the fortifications that once protected these islands from pirates. The Azorean culture is also deeply influenced by the sea, with festivals and traditions that reflect the community's bond with the ocean.

The religious festivals, particularly the "Festas do Espírito Santo," involve colorful parades and ceremonies that are a treat for visitors. These festivals are held from April through September and are a vital part of the Azorean calendar, providing insight into the spiritual and community life of the islands.

Local Delicacies and Cuisine

The cuisine of the Azores is as varied as its landscapes, heavily based on seafood, dairy products, and locally grown produce. São Jorge cheese, a spicy, semi-hard cheese that has been produced for over 500 years, is a must-try for food lovers. Cozido das Furnas, a stew that includes a variety of meats and vegetables cooked by volcanic steam underground, offers a taste that can't be found anywhere else in the world.

Adventurous Activities

The islands are a paradise for adventurers and nature lovers. Whale watching is a popular activity, with the Azores being one of the best places in the world to observe whales and dolphins in their natural habitat. The rich marine life also makes it an excellent spot for diving, particularly around the Formigas Islets, where divers can explore shipwrecks and vibrant underwater ecosystems.

Hiking is another activity that draws visitors. Trails like the ones in Terceira's "Misterios Negros" take you through ancient lava fields and lush forests, offering both a challenging trek and the reward of unparalleled natural beauty.

Travel Tips and Practical Information

To fully enjoy the Azores, it's best to plan your visit between April and October when the weather is most favorable for outdoor activities. Each island has its airport, with regular flights from Lisbon and Porto, and inter-island connections primarily operated by SATA Air Açores. Travelers can also use the ferry services provided by Atlanticoline during the warmer months, which is a great way to hop between islands and see the archipelago from a different perspective.

Accommodations in the Azores range from luxury hotels to charming bed and breakfasts, with options to suit every budget. For an authentic experience, consider staying in a traditional Azorean house, available for rent throughout the islands.

A Brief History

Discovery and Settlement

The Azores were officially discovered in the 1430s by Portuguese naviga-tors. Gonçalo Velho Cabral, a Portuguese explorer, is often credited with the discovery of Santa Maria and São Miguel, the first two islands of the archipelago. By the 1450s, settlers from various regions of Portugal, along with Flemish, Italian, and French immigrants, began populating the islands. These settlers brought with them the agricultural practices that would shape the Azorean landscape, introducing crops such as wheat, grape vines, and sugar cane.

Strategic Importance in the 16th and 17th Centuries

Due to their strategic location in the Atlantic Ocean, the Azores played a pivotal role in transatlantic navigation. The islands served as a stopping point for Portuguese ships returning from Africa, India, and the Americas, laden with goods and riches. This made them a target for pirates and privateers, leading to the construction of forts and defensive systems, remnants of which can still be seen today, particularly in Angra do Heroísmo on Terceira Island. Angra was also a key point in the spread of Christianity, with the Jesuits establishing a strong presence on the island.

The Azores and the Liberal Wars

The 19th century brought turmoil to Portugal, and the Azores were not spared. The islands were crucial during the Portuguese Liberal Wars, with the city of Angra do Heroísmo again playing a significant role. In 1829, it was named a city by Queen Maria II, and it became the temporary capital of the Portuguese kingdom loyal to her cause against her uncle who claimed the throne. The victory of the liberals marked a turning point in the history of Portugal and affirmed the strategic political importance of the Azores.

The 20th Century and Emigration

Throughout the 20th century, the Azores experienced significant emigration, particularly to the United States and Canada. The harsh economic conditions and volcanic eruptions, such as the Capelinhos eruption on Faial Island in 1957-58, led many Azoreans to seek better lives overseas. This migration has created a vibrant Azorean diaspora and has linked Azorean culture closely with North American influences.

Azorean Autonomy and Modern Identity

The latter half of the 20th century saw significant political changes for the Azores. In 1976, following the Carnation Revolution in Portugal which overthrew decades of dictatorship, the Azores achieved political autonomy. This autonomy allowed for the development of a regional government capable of addressing the unique geographic and economic challenges of the archipelago.

Today, the Azores are known for their significant contributions to environmental sustainability and conservation. The islands are a pioneer in using renewable energy sources, and efforts to preserve the unique flora and fauna of the archipelago are robust. The landscape is marked by UNESCO-designated biosphere reserves and nature parks that reflect a commitment to protecting the environment.

Cultural Evolution

The culture of the Azores is a rich blend of the traditions brought by its early settlers and the modern influences brought back by emigrants returning to the islands. This is evident in the festivals, cuisine, and daily life on the islands. The Festas do Espírito Santo, which are celebrated throughout the islands, are a vivid example of how historical religious practices have been preserved and adapted over centuries. These festivals involve processions, coronations, and the distribution of food, which highlight the community spirit and generosity that define Azorean culture.

The history of the Azores is a story of resilience and adaptation. From their role in global maritime routes to their emergence as a self-reliant and culturally rich archipelago, the islands have navigated the challenges of their geographic isolation to forge a unique identity. Visitors to the Azores can not only revel in the natural beauty of the islands but can also appreciate the depth of history that has shaped this remarkable place. The fortifications, museums, and cultural festivals provide not just entertainment but also a deeper understanding of the enduring spirit of the Azorean people.

For travelers interested in exploring historical sites, Angra do Heroísmo is an essential stop. The city's fortifications, including the Fortress of São João Baptista, and the Angra do Heroísmo Museum, located at Rua da Esperança, provide insights into the military and cultural history of the islands. Entry to the museum is typically around 3 euros, offering travelers a budget-friendly way to experience the rich history of the Azores firsthand.

The Azores Today: Culture and Contemporary Life

Cultural Expressions

Cultural festivals play a central role in Azorean life, with each island hosting a variety of events that showcase local traditions, music, and dance. One of the most prominent is the Festas do Espírito Santo, celebrated from April to September across the islands. These festivals feature colorful parades, traditional music, and the unique "sopas do Espírito Santo," a soup that is shared among the community. Visitors can experience these festivities in towns like Ponta Delgada on São Miguel, where local halls, known as "impérios," open their doors to the public.

Another vital aspect of Azorean culture is its handicrafts, especially the renowned Azorean lace and ceramics. In cities like Vila Franca do Campo, tourists can visit workshops like Cerâmica Vieira (Rua da Cruz, 10, Vila Franca do Campo), where they can watch artisans at work and purchase handmade pieces. Prices for these crafts start at around 15 euros, offering a tangible piece of Azorean artistry to take home.

Lifestyle

Daily life in the Azores is closely tied to the islands' natural surroundings. Farming and fishing are still vital to the local economy and culinary traditions. The Azores are famous for their dairy products, particularly the cheese from São Jorge. Visitors can tour local farms, such as Quinta dos Açores (Estrada Regional, Angra do Heroísmo, São Jorge), to see the production process and sample fresh cheese, with tours costing approximately 10 euros.

The sea is another cornerstone of Azorean life. In coastal towns like Horta on Faial Island, maritime activities are a daily routine. The Horta Marina (Avenida 25 de Abril, Horta) is a hub for sailors crossing the Atlantic, and its walls, painted by visitors from around the world, tell stories of maritime journeys.

Modern Innovations

While tradition forms the backbone of the Azorean lifestyle, modern innovations have also found their place. Renewable energy, particularly geothermal, is a significant focus, reflecting the islands' commitment to sustainability. The Azores are aiming to become carbon-neutral, with projects like the geothermal power plant in Ribeira Grande (Lugar da Ribeira Grande, São Miguel) leading the way. Visitors can join guided tours of the facility to learn about geothermal energy, with entry fees around 5 euros.

In terms of connectivity, the Azores have embraced digital technology to enhance tourism and local life. Wi-Fi is widely available, and tech hubs like Terceira Tech Island (Parque de Ciência e Tecnologia da Terceira, Praia da Vitória) offer spaces for digital nomads and startups, showcasing the islands' progressive approach to technology and business.

Blending Tradition and Modernity

The Azores' unique blend of old and new is perhaps best illustrated in their culinary scene. Traditional dishes, like the aforementioned cozido das Furnas, are prepared using volcanic steam, while contemporary Azorean restaurants incorporate international influences to create innovative cuisine. Restaurants such as Restaurante Alcides (Rua Hintze Ribeiro, Ponta Delgada), known for its fusion of traditional and modern techniques, offer dishes starting at around 20 euros.

Cultural and Social Development

The Azores are also seeing a cultural renaissance, with investments in the arts and education. The Arquipélago – Contemporary Arts Center (Rua

Adolfo Coutinho de Medeiros, Ribeira Grande) is a prime example, hosting exhibitions and workshops that highlight both Azorean and international artists.

Today, the Azores represent a society that respects and preserves its historical roots while steadily marching towards a sustainable and innovative future. This balance makes the archipelago not just a travel destination but a living museum of cultural preservation and modernization. Visitors leave with a profound appreciation of how the Azores have navigated the complexities of maintaining cultural identity in a changing world, making it a truly unique place to experience.

Azores at a Glance

The Azores, a captivating archipelago situated in the mid-Atlantic, is composed of nine volcanic islands that are an autonomous region of Portugal. Renowned for their breathtaking landscapes, rich marine life, and vibrant culture, the islands offer a peaceful retreat with a strikingly beautiful backdrop.

Geography

The nine islands are spread over a vast area of the Atlantic Ocean, divided into three groups:

- The Eastern Group includes São Miguel, the largest and most populous island, and Santa Maria, known for its warm beaches.
- The Central Group comprises Terceira, known for its historical sites; Graciosa, with its tranquil pastures; São Jorge, famous for its steep cliffs and cheese; Pico, dominated by Portugal's highest mountain; and Faial, known for its sailors' marina.
- The Western Group consists of Flores and Corvo, remote islands known for their dramatic landscapes and abundant birdlife.

Climate

The Azores experience a mild maritime climate. Temperatures vary slightly throughout the year, from cooler, wet winters to warm, humid summers. The ocean significantly influences the climate, keeping the islands temperate and helping to avoid extreme weather, making the Azores a year-round destination.

Culture

The culture of the Azores is a rich amalgam influenced by the settlers from mainland Portugal and other European countries. Festivals, religious ceremonies, and traditional dances play a crucial role in community life, reflecting the deep-seated spirit of the islands. The most famous celebration is the Festas do Espírito Santo, involving processions, crowning ceremonies, and communal feasts.

Economy

The economy of the Azores is primarily based on agriculture, dairy farming (particularly cheese production), and fishing. In recent years, tourism has grown to be a significant part of the economy, supported by the islands' natural beauty and unique geological sights. The local government actively promotes sustainable practices to preserve the environment while encouraging economic development.

Biodiversity and Natural Environment

The islands are a hotspot for biodiversity, boasting a wide range of endemic species, both terrestrial and marine. The lush, verdant landscapes are home to unique flora and fauna, while the surrounding waters are a key breeding and feeding ground for whales, dolphins, and other marine species. Several nature reserves and protected areas, such as the UNESCO World Biosphere Reserve on Graciosa, safeguard these natural treasures.

Transportation

Connectivity between the islands is maintained through a network of airports and ports. Regular flights link the islands to each other and to mainland Europe, primarily through Ponta Delgada Airport on São Miguel. Ferry services provide an alternative mode of transport, especially in the summer months, offering scenic journeys between the islands.

Tourism

Tourism in the Azores is centered around the natural environment.

Activities such as whale watching, hiking, diving, and bird watching are particularly popular. The islands also offer a range of accommodations, from luxury hotels to local guesthouses, catering to diverse tastes and budgets.

Gastronomy

Azorean cuisine reflects the islands' volcanic origins and maritime culture. Seafood is prominently featured, along with meats and vegetables that are often cooked using geothermal heat. Local cheeses, particularly from São Jorge, are highly prized. The regional wines and teas, cultivated in the unique climatic conditions of the Azores, provide distinct flavors that are a delight to explore.

Essential Information

Best Times to Visit

Weather Patterns Across the Year

The Azores are characterized by their mild, humid weather with relatively stable temperatures throughout the year. The climate varies slightly between the islands due to their geographical dispersion.

Winter (December to February)

- Temperatures: Average lows of 12°C (54°F) and highs of 17°C (63°F).
- Weather: Winters are rainy, especially in January and February, with the highest precipitation of the year. Wind speeds can also be higher during this time.
- Travel Recommendation: Winter is less crowded, making it ideal for those seeking solitude. The lush landscapes following the rains are vibrant. Rates for accommodations are generally lower.

Spring (March to May)

- Temperatures: Gradual warming with averages from 14°C (57°F) to 18°C (64°F).
- Weather: Rainfall decreases, and the islands begin to bloom, creating spectacular floral displays, particularly hydrangeas and azaleas.

- Travel Recommendation: This is an excellent time for hiking and enjoying the outdoors. Birdwatching is particularly rewarding as migratory species stop over in the Azores.

Summer (June to August)

- Temperatures: Warmest months with temperatures ranging from 18°C (64°F) to 25°C (77°F).
- Weather: Summer is the driest season in the Azores, featuring longer days and sunnier skies.
- Travel Recommendation: Ideal for beach activities, whale watching, and attending local festivals. Prices peak due to the high demand, especially in July and August.

Autumn (September to November)

- Temperatures: Mild, with averages similar to spring, slowly cooling from 20°C (68°F) to 16°C (61°F).
- Weather: Rainfall increases towards the end of autumn, but early September still offers plenty of sunny days.
- Travel Recommendation: The sea remains warm enough for swimming in early autumn, and the decreasing number of tourists restores tranquility to popular spots.

Seasonal Highlights and Events

Visiting the Azores is also about experiencing its rich cultural tapestry through local events and festivals, which reflect the history and spirit of the islands.

Spring

- **Azores Fringe Festival** (June): An international arts festival that takes places across the islands, showcasing music, visual arts, and performances. Visitors can enjoy this cultural feast in venues like Teatro Micaelense in Ponta Delgada (Address: Largo de São João, Ponta Delgada).

Summer

- **Festas de São João** (June): Vibrant street festivals in Angra do Heroísmo, Terceira, celebrating Saint John with parades, traditional dances, and games.
- **Whale Watching Season**: Peaks in the summer, when migrating cetaceans pass by the islands. Operators like Futurismo Azores Whale Watching (Address: Rua dos Baleeiros, Ponta Delgada) offer tours starting at €55.

Autumn

- **Santa Maria Blues Festival** (July): Renowned blues festival attracting international artists, held in Vila do Porto, Santa Maria. Tickets typically cost around €20.
- **Grape Harvest** (September): Participate in grape harvests and wine tasting events on Pico Island. The Adega Cooperativa do Pico (Address: Areia Larga, Madalena) is open for tours and tastings.

Winter

- **Christmas Festivities** (December): Local markets and celebrations, including midnight masses and traditional concerts, are prevalent. The Ponta Delgada city center is adorned with lights and decorations, creating a festive atmosphere.

Practical Information for Visitors

When planning a trip to the Azores, consider both the climatic conditions and the events you wish to attend. Booking in advance is advisable, especially during the peak summer months. Travelers can reach the Azores by air with direct flights from Europe and North America to Ponta Delgada Airport (Main airport address: 9500-749 São Miguel, Azores). Local transportation options include rental cars and inter-island flights operated by SATA Air Açores.

Entry Requirements, Customs Regulations, and Tips for Smooth Entry into the Azores

Entry Requirements
For EU Citizens:

- **Identification:** EU citizens can enter the Azores with either a passport or a national ID card.
- **Duration of Stay:** There are no restrictions on the length of stay for EU citizens within the Schengen Area.

For Non-EU Citizens:

- **Visa Requirements:** Non-EU citizens from countries that do not have visa exemption agreements with the Schengen Area will need to obtain a Schengen visa. This visa allows a stay of up to 90 days within a 180-day period.
- **Application Process:** Visa applications should be submitted to the nearest Portuguese consulate or embassy. The process typically involves submitting a visa form, passport-sized photos, travel itinerary, proof of accommodation, travel insurance, and a cover letter explaining the purpose of the visit.
- **Cost:** A standard short-stay Schengen visa costs approximately €80 for adults and €40 for children aged 6-12. It is free for children under six

years old.

Passport Validity:

- All travelers should have a passport valid for at least three months beyond their planned departure date from the Schengen Area.

Customs Regulations

Understanding the customs regulations is crucial for bringing goods into the Azores, especially for those who plan to bring specific items with them.

Duty-Free Allowance for Non-EU Travelers:

- **Tobacco Products:** 200 cigarettes or 100 cigarillos or 50 cigars or 250g of smoking tobacco.
- **Alcohol:** 4 liters of non-sparkling wine and 16 liters of beer, plus 1 liter of spirits over 22% alcohol volume or 2 liters of alcoholic beverages less than 22%.
- **Other Goods:** Up to a value of €430 for air and sea travelers.

Restricted and Prohibited Items:

- **Food Products:** Importing meat and dairy products from outside the EU is generally prohibited without a license.
- **Plants and Plant Products:** Strict controls are in place to prevent the spread of pests and diseases. A phytosanitary certificate is required for certain plant products.
- **Medications:** Travelers bringing prescribed medication should carry a doctor's prescription and ensure that the medication is in its original packaging.

Tips for a Smooth Entry

To ensure a hassle-free entry into the Azores, travelers can follow these tips:

1. **Complete Documentation:** Ensure all required documents, including visas, are complete and valid before departure.
2. **Declare Goods at Customs:** Be honest and clear when declaring goods at customs to avoid delays and possible fines.
3. **Check Luggage Restrictions:** Familiarize yourself with airline and airport regulations regarding luggage to avoid issues at security checkpoints.
4. **Health and Travel Insurance:** Possessing travel insurance that covers health, accidents, and unexpected trip cancellations is highly advisable.
5. **Contact Information:** Keep the contact information of your country's embassy or consulate in Portugal in case of emergencies.

Contact Information for Further Assistance:

- **Serviço de Estrangeiros e Fronteiras (SEF):** For visa and residency inquiries, contact SEF at Avenida António Augusto de Aguiar 20, 1069-119 Lisboa, Portugal. Phone: +351 21 711 50 00.
- **Portuguese Embassy or Consulate:** Locate the nearest embassy or consulate via the Portuguese Ministry of Foreign Affairs website for specific national advice.

Staying Healthy and Safe: Local Advice
Health Precautions

- **Vaccinations:** Before traveling to the Azores, ensure your routine vaccinations are up to date. These include measles-mumps-rubella (MMR), diphtheria-tetanus-pertussis, varicella (chickenpox), polio, and your yearly flu shot. Hepatitis A and B vaccinations are recommended due to the potential for transmission through contaminated food, water, or close contact with the local population.

- **Medical Insurance:** Secure comprehensive travel health insurance that covers medical evacuation. Verify that your insurance plan is accepted in the Azores and covers activities you plan to engage in, like hiking or diving.
- **Sun Exposure:** The Azores can have deceptively strong UV levels, particularly in summer. Use a broad-spectrum sunscreen with an SPF of at least 30, wear protective clothing, and limit sun exposure between 10 AM and 4 PM when the sun is strongest.
- **Water Safety:** Tap water in the Azores is generally safe to drink. However, those with sensitive stomachs may prefer bottled water to avoid any potential issues.

Safety Tips

- **Natural Hazards:** The Azores are located in a geologically active area, meaning volcanic activity and earthquakes are possible, though rare. Familiarize yourself with local emergency procedures and follow any advice or instructions provided by local authorities.
- **Driving:** If you choose to drive, be aware that roads can be narrow and winding, especially in rural areas. Ensure you have a valid driver's license and understand local traffic laws. Use caution when driving in foggy conditions, common in the Azores.
- **Hiking Safety:** When hiking, always inform someone of your plans and expected return time. Stick to marked trails and check weather conditions before setting out. Wear suitable footwear and carry sufficient water and snacks.

Accessing Medical Care

Hospitals and Health Centers: The Azores have well-equipped hospitals and health centers:

- **Hospital do Divino Espírito Santo (Ponta Delgada, São Miguel):** This is the largest hospital in the Azores, providing emergency and specialist services. Address: Largo da Esperança, 9500-461 Ponta Delgada. Phone: +351 296 203 000.
- **Hospital de Santo Espírito da Ilha Terceira (Angra do Heroísmo, Terceira):** Offers comprehensive medical services. Address: Canada do Barreiro, 9700-045 Angra do Heroísmo. Phone: +351 295 403 200.

Pharmacies: Pharmacies are readily available in major towns and cities. Pharmacists can offer advice on minor ailments and sell over-the-counter medication. Look for a green cross sign indicating a pharmacy.

Emergency Services: In case of emergency, dial 112 for immediate assistance. This number can be used to contact police, fire services, and medical help.

Travel Health Clinics: For travelers needing health services or vaccinations, travel health clinics are available in larger towns. These clinics provide pre-travel immunizations and health advice.

Safety in Public Areas: While the Azores are generally safe, exercise usual precautions:

- Avoid carrying large amounts of cash.
- Keep valuables out of sight to prevent theft.
- Be aware of your surroundings, especially at night.

Marine Safety: When participating in water sports or swimming, always follow local guidelines and safety instructions. Be aware of the local sea conditions and currents, and never swim alone.

Journey to the Azores

Air Routes

International and Regional Airports
The Azores boast three main international airports, which serve as gateways to the islands and hubs for inter-island flights.

João Paulo II Airport (Ponta Delgada Airport) - São Miguel Island

- **Address:** 9500-749 São Miguel, Azores, Portugal.
- **Contact:** +351 296 205 400
- **Facilities:** ATMs, car rentals, taxi services, shops, restaurants, and free Wi-Fi.
- **Airlines:** This airport hosts a range of international flights from Europe and North America. Airlines such as SATA/Azores Airlines, TAP Air Portugal, and Ryanair offer direct connections to major cities like Lisbon, Porto, Boston, and Toronto.
- **Tips for Arrival:** Upon landing, travelers can exchange currency at the airport and avail themselves of tourist information services to assist with any immediate travel needs.

Lajes Field (Terceira Airport) - Terceira Island

- **Address:** 9760-251 Lajes, Praia da Vitória, Terceira, Azores, Portugal.

- **Contact:** +351 295 545 454
- **Facilities:** Includes basic amenities such as cafes, car rental services, and a small duty-free shop.
- **Airlines:** Handles flights from major Portuguese cities and limited international flights, mostly seasonal charters.

Horta Airport - Faial Island

- **Address:** 9900-321 Castelo Branco, Horta, Faial, Azores, Portugal.
- **Contact:** +351 292 943 511
- **Facilities:** Offers essential services including car rentals, taxis, and snack bars.
- **Airlines:** Primarily serves inter-island flights with some connections to mainland Portugal.

Tips for Booking Flights

- **Early Reservations:** Book your flights to the Azores well in advance, especially if traveling during peak tourist season (June through August). Early booking often secures better rates and more flexible travel options.
- **Compare Prices:** Use flight comparison websites to find the best deals and routes. Consider flying into one of mainland Portugal's airports, such as Lisbon or Porto, and then booking a separate flight to the Azores.
- **Check Airline Promotions:** Both SATA/Azores Airlines and TAP Air Portugal frequently offer promotions for flights to and from the islands. Signing up for their newsletters can keep you informed about possible discounts.
- **Consider Stopovers:** Some airlines offer free stopovers in Lisbon or Porto, allowing a multi-destination trip without additional airfare costs.

What to Expect Upon Landing

- **Customs and Immigration:** If you're arriving from outside the Schengen Area, you'll need to go through passport control. EU citizens can use automated gates, while others will queue for manual passport checks.
- **Baggage Claim:** Baggage claim areas in Azorean airports are typically close to the arrival gates. Trolleys are usually available for free.
- **Transport from Airport:** All main airports in the Azores offer public buses, taxis, and rental cars. Taxi stands are located outside the arrival areas, and most taxi drivers speak English. Rental car reservations can be made in advance or upon arrival but booking ahead is recommended during busy periods.
- **Local Information:** Tourist information booths are found in the main airports. They provide maps, brochures, and helpful advice for navigating the islands.

Estimated Costs

- **Flights from Lisbon to Ponta Delgada:** Round-trip flights typically range from €100 to €300 depending on the season.
- **Taxis from Ponta Delgada Airport to downtown:** Approximately €10 to €15.
- **Car Rentals:** Starting from €40 per day depending on the vehicle and rental duration.

Sea Travel: Ferries Between the Islands

Ferry Operators and Routes

The primary operator for inter-island ferry services in the Azores is Atlânticoline. They offer seasonal services covering all nine islands, ensuring connectivity through various routes:

Main Routes:

- **Horta (Faial) to Pico:** This is one of the most frequented routes due to the proximity of the islands.
- **Ponta Delgada (São Miguel) to Vila do Porto (Santa Maria):** Operates mainly in the summer months, linking the two largest islands of the group.
- **Angra do Heroísmo (Terceira) to Velas (São Jorge):** A crucial link for accessing São Jorge from Terceira.

Less Frequent Routes:

- **Flores to Corvo:** A vital connection between the two westernmost islands, especially popular with bird watchers and nature enthusiasts.

Schedules and Seasonality

Ferry schedules vary significantly between summer and winter due to the maritime conditions and demand:

- **Summer Season (May to September):** During these months, Atlânticoline increases the frequency of their trips to accommodate the higher number of tourists. Schedules are usually available by early April.
- **Winter Season (October to April):** Services are reduced, and some routes may not operate, particularly those susceptible to harsh weather conditions.

Booking Tickets

- **Advance Booking:** It is advisable to book tickets in advance, especially during the summer months. Tickets can be purchased online, through Atlânticoline's website, or at their ticket offices located at major ports.

Ticket Offices: Key locations include:

- **Ponta Delgada Maritime Terminal:** Avenida Infante Dom Henrique, 9500-150 Ponta Delgada. Contact: +351 296 288 257
- **Horta Maritime Terminal:** Largo Dr. Manuel de Arriaga, 9900-026 Horta. Contact: +351 292 208 300
- **Angra do Heroísmo Maritime Terminal:** Porto das Pipas, 9700-154 Angra do Heroísmo. Contact: +351 295 401 700

Online Booking: Visit Atlânticoline's website for schedules and online ticketing. Payment can be made via major credit cards.

Costs

- **Ticket Prices:** Costs vary depending on the route, season, and class (e.g., tourist class or first class). A one-way ticket for the Horta to Pico route can range from €6 to €12 in tourist class.
- **Discounts:** Discounts may be available for seniors, children, and residents of the Azores.

Travel Tips

- **Check Weather Conditions:** Sea conditions can affect ferry operations, particularly in winter. It's wise to check weather forecasts and stay informed about any service changes.
- **Arrive Early:** For international travelers and those with vehicles, arriving at least one hour before departure is recommended. This ensures ample time for boarding and any last-minute formalities.
- **Luggage and Facilities:** Most ferries allow a generous luggage allowance and are equipped with cafeterias and comfortable seating areas. Larger ferries also offer cabins for longer journeys.
- **Scenic Views:** Choose seating on the upper decks for the best scenic

views during your trip. The journey between the islands can be breathtaking, with opportunities to see dolphins or whales.

Accessibilities: Insights for Travelers with Disabilities or Special Needs

Transportation
Airports:

- All major airports in the Azores, including João Paulo II Airport in Ponta Delgada and Lajes Field in Terceira, are equipped with ramps, accessible restrooms, and dedicated assistance services. It is advisable to contact the airport in advance to arrange any necessary assistance upon arrival and departure.
- **Contacts:**
- João Paulo II Airport, Ponta Delgada: +351 296 205 400
- Lajes Field, Terceira: +351 295 545 454

Ferries:

- Atlânticoline, the primary ferry operator, provides accessible options on their larger vessels, which include ramps, adapted restrooms, and priority boarding for travelers with reduced mobility. Booking in advance allows the staff to prepare for any specific requirements.
- **Contact:** Atlânticoline Customer Service: +351 292 242 400

Public Buses:

- Major towns on the islands, such as Ponta Delgada and Angra do

Heroísmo, offer buses equipped with low-entry platforms for easier access. However, not all bus routes may have fully accessible buses, so checking with the local bus companies before planning day trips is recommended.

- **Contacts:**
- Ponta Delgada Urban Transport: +351 296 288 028
- Angra Public Transit: +351 295 206 700

Accommodations

Many hotels and resorts in the Azores have rooms adapted for guests with disabilities, featuring wider doors, grab bars in the bathrooms, and emergency alert systems. Here are a couple of well-regarded options:

Terra Nostra Garden Hotel (São Miguel): Offers rooms designed for wheelchair users, complete with roll-in showers and appropriate support fittings.

- **Address:** Rua Padre José Jacinto Botelho, 5, 9675-061 Furnas, São Miguel
- **Contact:** +351 296 549 090

Hotel do Caracol (Terceira): Features accessible rooms and public areas, along with pool access for guests with mobility impairments.

- **Address:** Estrada Regional 1, 1, Silveira, 9700-193 Angra do Heroísmo, Terceira
- **Contact:** +351 295 402 600

Tourist Attractions

The Azores are improving accessibility at their key tourist sites. Here's what to expect at some popular spots:

Furnas Monitoring and Research Center (São Miguel): Accessible paths and informative displays are available for all visitors. Staff are trained to assist guests with special needs.

- **Address:** Rua da Água Quente, 9675-040 Furnas, São Miguel
- **Contact:** +351 296 584 256

Capelinhos Volcano Interpretation Centre (Faial): The center offers accessible entrances and elevators, making the exhibitions reachable for everyone.

- **Address:** Farol dos Capelinhos, 9900-301 Capelo, Faial
- **Contact:** +351 292 200 470

Dining

Restaurants across the islands are increasingly aware of the need for accessibility. Most of the newer or recently renovated establishments offer at least ground-level access and spacious seating to accommodate wheelchairs:

- **Restaurante Atlântida (São Miguel):** Not only is the dining area accessible, but the staff are also trained to assist guests with special dietary needs or physical disabilities.
- **Address:** Avenida Infante Dom Henrique, 9500-769 São Miguel
- **Contact:** +351 296 282 677

Recreational Activities

For those interested in experiencing the natural beauty of the Azores up close, several tour operators specialize in accessible adventure tourism, offering custom tours tailored to the needs of travelers with disabilities:

- **Azores for All:** Pioneers in accessible tourism in the archipelago, offering tailored tours that include bird watching, city tours, and nature walks with accessible paths.
- **Address:** Rua da Pranchinha, 92, Ponta Delgada, São Miguel
- **Contact:** +351 296 628 522

Navigating the Islands

Getting Your Bearings

Key Geographical Features

The Azores archipelago consists of nine volcanic islands spread over three distinct groups:

Eastern Group:

- **São Miguel:** The largest island, known for its dramatic volcanic landscapes, hot springs, and lush greenery. Key features include the Sete Cidades caldera and the Furnas Valley.
- **Santa Maria:** Famous for its white sandy beaches and dry warm climate, a contrast to the other islands. Points of interest include the Barreiro da Faneca and the historical town of Vila do Porto.

Central Group:

- **Terceira:** Known for its historical towns like Angra do Heroísmo, a UNESCO World Heritage Site. The island features a mix of volcanic craters and rugged coastlines.
- **Graciosa:** Characterized by its tranquil scenery and windmills. Key sites include the Furna do Enxofre, a rare geological cave.
- **São Jorge:** Renowned for its steep cliffs and fajãs (flat coastal areas

formed by lava flows). Notable spots are Fajã do Santo Cristo and Fajã dos Cubres.

- **Pico:** Dominated by Mount Pico, Portugal's highest mountain. The island is also noted for its vineyards, protected under UNESCO.
- **Faial:** Known for the Capelinhos Volcano and the marina in Horta, a popular stopping point for transatlantic yachts.

Western Group:

- **Flores:** Celebrated for its abundance of flowers and waterfalls, including the famous Poço da Alagoinha.
- **Corvo:** The smallest island, known for its large volcanic caldera and birdwatching opportunities, particularly at Lagoa do Caldeirão.

Obtaining Maps

Maps are crucial for navigating the Azores, whether you're driving, hiking, or exploring towns.

Here's how to obtain them:

Tourist Offices: Available on all major islands, tourist offices provide free maps that highlight key attractions, roads, and trails.

Locations include Ponta Delgada on São Miguel and Angra do Heroísmo on Terceira.

Contacts:

- São Miguel Tourist Office: +351 296 308 400 (Address: Avenida Infante Dom Henrique, 9500-150 Ponta Delgada)
- Terceira Tourist Office: +351 295 403 800 (Address: Rua de São João, 9700-182 Angra do Heroísmo)

Online Resources: Prior to your visit, download digital maps from reputable sources such as Google Maps or the official Azores tourism website. These maps are useful for pre-trip planning and can be used on smartphones and GPS devices.

Local Bookstores: For detailed topographical maps, visit local bookstores. These maps are especially useful for hikers and outdoor enthusiasts. Prices typically range from €5 to €15.

Using Maps Effectively

- **Understand Symbols:** Familiarize yourself with common map symbols and terms used in the Azores. Knowing these can help you identify key landmarks, types of roads, and trails.
- **Plan Your Route:** Before setting out each day, plan your route. Consider the time it takes to travel between points of interest, especially on winding mountain roads or hiking trails.
- **Check Weather Conditions:** Weather can impact visibility and access, especially in higher altitudes like Pico's summit or coastal trails. Use maps alongside weather apps to plan safe routes.
- **Ask Locals:** Locals can provide updates on road conditions, trail closures, or less-known spots worth visiting. Combine their advice with your maps for the best experience.

Local Transport: Buses, Taxis, and Car Hire

Buses

Buses in the Azores provide an economical way to travel, particularly within the larger islands like São Miguel and Terceira. Each island has its own bus service, offering routes that cover most major communities and tourist attractions.

São Miguel: Minibus Azores operates extensive routes around the island, connecting Ponta Delgada with remote areas.

- **Contact:** +351 296 288 028

Main Hub: Avenida Infante Dom Henrique, Ponta Delgada

- **Cost:** Single fares start at about €1.50, with day passes available around €4.00.

Terceira: Public buses run by Cooperativa Praia da Vitória offer connections between major towns.

- **Contact:** +351 295 540 500

Main Hub: Rua da Sé, Angra do Heroísmo

- **Cost:** Fares vary by distance, generally around €1.00 to €3.00 per trip.

Bus schedules can be limited, especially on weekends and holidays, so planning ahead is crucial. Schedules and maps are usually available at tourist offices and online.

Taxis

Taxis are a convenient option for direct travel, especially for areas not well-served by public transport.

- **Availability:** Taxis are readily available at airports, hotels, and central locations. They can be hailed on the street or booked via phone.
- **Cost:** Starting fares are about €3.50, with additional charges per kilometer around €0.50. Prices increase at night and on weekends.
- **Contacts for Taxi Services:**
- São Miguel: Autocoope Ponta Delgada, +351 296 302 530

THE AZORES TRAVEL GUIDE 2025

- Terceira: Taxis Terceira, +351 295 333 333

Car Hire

Renting a car offers the most flexibility for exploring the Azores at your own pace. Car rental agencies are available at airports and major towns.

- **Requirements:** Drivers need a valid driver's license from their home country, and an international driving permit is recommended for non-EU citizens. The minimum age to rent a car is typically 21, with a driving experience of at least one year.
- **Cost:** Daily rental rates start at about €30 for a basic car, with prices varying based on the car model and rental duration.
- **Insurance:** Basic insurance is included, but it's advisable to consider additional coverage for peace of mind.
- **Popular Car Rental Agencies:**
- Ilha Verde Rent a Car, +351 296 684 360 (São Miguel Airport)
- Rent-a-Car Oceano, +351 295 516 424 (Terceira Airport)

Driving Tips

- **Road Conditions:** While main roads are generally in good condition, many secondary roads are narrow and winding. Extra caution is advised, especially in rural areas.
- **Fuel:** Gas stations are widespread in populated areas but can be sparse in remote regions. Always keep the tank reasonably full when venturing into less inhabited parts of the islands.
- **Parking:** Public parking is available in larger towns and near major attractions, often free or for a nominal fee.

Travel Tips: Moving Between and Within the Islands

Planning Your Travel
 Understand the Geography:

- Familiarize yourself with the layout of the islands. São Miguel, the largest island, serves as a central hub, with frequent flights and ferries to other islands. Knowing the proximity and accessibility of each island can help you plan an efficient itinerary.

Check Transport Schedules in Advance:

- Transport schedules, especially for ferries and flights, can vary by season. Checking schedules ahead of time allows you to book tickets early and avoid last-minute inconveniences.

Useful Contacts:

- SATA Airline for inter-island flights: +351 296 209 720
- Atlânticoline for ferry schedules: +351 292 242 400

Accommodation Locations:

- Choose accommodations that are centrally located to the activities and areas you plan to explore. This reduces travel time and costs.
- Example: In Ponta Delgada (São Miguel), stay near the city center or along coastal roads for easy access to beaches, restaurants, and transport services.

Inter-Island Travel
 Choosing Your Mode of Transport:

- **Flights:** Ideal for quick transfers between islands, especially those further apart like Flores and Corvo.
- **Ferries:** Best used during the summer months for scenic and cost-effective travel. Not all islands are connected daily, so planning is essential.

Booking Strategies:

- Book flights and ferries as soon as your travel dates are confirmed to secure the best fares and availability.
- Consider multi-island packages offered by airlines and ferry companies, which can be cost-effective for extensive explorations.

Travel Within Islands
Car Rentals:

- Renting a car offers the most flexibility for exploring the islands at your pace. Rental agencies are available at airports and major towns.
- **Average Cost:** €30-€50 per day, depending on the car model and rental duration.
- **Driving Tips:** Always have a map or GPS, as cell service can be unreliable in remote areas.

Public Transport:

- Buses are available on the larger islands like São Miguel and Terceira but may be less frequent on smaller islands.
- **Tip:** Obtain a bus schedule from local tourist offices or download one from municipal websites.

Taxis and Private Transfers:

- Convenient for direct journeys or when public transport isn't available.
- **Cost:** Fares typically start at €4, with additional charges based on distance. Agree on a fare before starting your journey to avoid surprises.

Packing and Preparation
Weather-Appropriate Clothing:

- The Azores can experience all four seasons in a day. Pack layers, including a waterproof jacket and sturdy walking shoes.

Travel Essentials:

- Bring chargers, adapters (European plug type), medications, and any specialized gear like hiking poles or snorkeling equipment.

Documentation:

- Keep digital and physical copies of important documents like your passport, driver's license, insurance cards, and booking confirmations.

Local Etiquette and Tips
Respect Nature:

- The natural beauty of the Azores is pristine. Always follow guidelines for conserving the environment, such as not littering and sticking to marked trails during hikes.

Engage with Locals:

- Locals appreciate when visitors take an interest in their culture and environment. Basic Portuguese phrases can go a long way in creating friendly interactions.

Safety and Emergency
Emergency Numbers:

- General Emergency (Police, Fire, Medical): 112
- Keep these numbers handy in your phone or written down in your travel kit.

Health Facilities:

- Know the location and contact details of the nearest health center or hospital from your stay location. Tourist offices can provide this information.

Where to Stay

Accommodation Types: From Hotels to Guesthouse

Hotels

Hotels in the Azores range from high-end luxury to mid-range and budget options, catering to different tastes and budgets.

Luxury Hotels:

Terra Nostra Garden Hotel (São Miguel): Renowned for its geothermal pool and botanical gardens.

- **Address:** Rua Padre José Jacinto Botelho, 5, Furnas, São Miguel
- **Cost:** Rooms typically start at €200 per night.
- **Contact:** +351 296 549 090
- **Booking:** Direct through their website or via major hotel booking platforms.

The Azor Hotel (Ponta Delgada, São Miguel): Known for its modern design and ocean views.

- **Address:** Av. Dr. João Bosco Mota Amaral, Ponta Delgada, São Miguel
- **Cost:** Starting at €150 per night.

- **Contact:** +351 296 249 900

Mid-Range Hotels:

Hotel do Canal (Horta, Faial): Close to the marina with views of Pico Island.

- **Address:** Largo Dr. Manuel de Arriaga, Horta, Faial
- **Cost:** Around €100 per night.
- **Contact:** +351 292 202 120

Budget Hotels:

- **Hotel Canadiano** (Ponta Delgada, São Miguel): Affordable and centrally located.
- **Address:** Rua do Contador, Ponta Delgada, São Miguel
- **Cost:** Rooms from €70 per night.
- **Contact:** +351 296 630 000

Guesthouses and Bed & Breakfasts

Guesthouses and B&Bs offer a more personal touch, often family-run, providing a cozy, home-like atmosphere.

Quinta das Buganvílias (Faial): A charming guesthouse close to the airport.

- **Address:** Estrada do Aeroporto, Faial
- **Cost:** From €60 per night.

- **Contact:** +351 292 943 676

Casa Vitoriana (Ponta Delgada, São Miguel): Set in a historic building, offering a quaint stay.

- **Address:** Rua José do Canto, 9, Ponta Delgada, São Miguel
- **Cost:** Approximately €80 per night.
- **Contact:** +351 296 629 431

Rural Tourism and Eco-Resorts

For those interested in nature and sustainability, rural and eco-resorts provide an immersive experience.

Furnas Lake Villas (São Miguel): Eco-friendly villas in a stunning setting by Furnas Lake.

- **Address:** Estrada Regional do Sul, Furnas, São Miguel
- **Cost:** Starting at €120 per night.
- **Contact:** +351 296 584 107

Quinta de São Pedro (Vila do Porto, Santa Maria): A rural getaway offering organic gardens and traditional architecture.

- **Address:** Vila do Porto, Santa Maria
- **Cost:** Rooms start at €90 per night.
- **Contact:** +351 296 882 330

Hostels

For budget travelers, especially younger visitors or solo adventurers, hostels are an excellent option.

Pousada de Juventude (São Jorge): Affordable and social, great for meeting other travelers.

- **Address:** Caminho do Meio, São Jorge
- **Cost:** Beds from €15 per night.
- **Contact:** +351 295 432 324

The Nook Hostel (Ponta Delgada, São Miguel): Popular among backpackers.

- **Address:** Rua de Lisboa, Ponta Delgada, São Miguel
- **Cost:** €20 per night for a dorm bed.
- **Contact:** +351 296 717 171

Booking Tips

- **Book Early:** Especially during the peak season (June to August), it's advisable to book your accommodation well in advance.
- **Check Reviews:** Platforms like TripAdvisor and Google Reviews can provide insights from previous guests.
- **Consider Location:** Depending on your itinerary, choose a location that minimizes daily travel and maximizes convenience.

Luxury Resorts: Indulging in the Best

White Exclusive Suites & Villas (São Miguel)

Curled up on the cliffside with panoramic views of the Atlantic Ocean, White Exclusive Suites & Villas provides a serene escape that blends elegance with natural beauty. This resort is celebrated for its meticulous attention to detail, from the decor to the personalized services.

- **Address:** Rua da Rocha Quebrada, Lagoa, São Miguel
- **Cost:** Rooms typically start at €250 per night.
- **Features:** This resort offers suites and villas, each with ocean views, a gourmet restaurant on-site that specializes in local cuisine, a bar, an outdoor swimming pool, and a wellness area offering a range of spa treatments.
- **Contact:** +351 296 249 153
- **How to Get There:** Located approximately 20 minutes by car from Ponta Delgada Airport. Car rental or taxi service is recommended.

Terra Nostra Garden Hotel (São Miguel)

Renowned for its location within the Terra Nostra Botanical Park, this hotel is not only a stay but an experience. Guests have direct access to the park's famous thermal pools and lush gardens.

- **Address:** Rua Padre José Jacinto Botelho, 5, Furnas, São Miguel
- **Cost:** Prices start around €200 per night.
- **Features:** Includes access to the thermal pools, a world-class spa, an indoor pool, a restaurant serving dishes made from locally sourced ingredients, and elegantly furnished rooms with garden views.
- **Contact:** +351 296 549 090
- **How to Get There:** The hotel is about a 45-minute drive from Ponta Delgada Airport. Transportation options include taxis or pre-arranged hotel transfers.

The Azor Hotel (Ponta Delgada, São Miguel)

This modern hotel brings a touch of urban sophistication to the Azores, located right on the marina of Ponta Delgada, offering easy access to local attractions.

- **Address:** Av. Dr. João Bosco Mota Amaral, Ponta Delgada, São Miguel
- **Cost:** Starting from €150 per night.
- **Features:** Rooftop pool, spa, fitness center, and a restaurant with an emphasis on Azorean cuisine. The hotel also offers a casino, meeting rooms, and custom tour services for guests.
- **Contact:** +351 296 249 900
- **How to Get There:** Just a 10-minute drive from João Paulo II Airport, with taxis readily available for transfers.

Hotel Aldeia da Fonte (Pico)

Cliffside on the island of Pico, Hotel Aldeia da Fonte integrates naturally into its environment, making it a quiet retreat for nature lovers.

- **Address:** Caminho de Baixo, Lajes do Pico, Pico
- **Cost:** Room rates begin at around €120 per night.
- **Features:** Six volcanic stone houses cuddled among lush gardens, a sea access, a yoga pavilion, a fitness trail, and a restaurant focusing on healthy local foods.
- **Contact:** +351 292 679 500
- **How to Get There:** The hotel is approximately 35 minutes from Pico Airport. Renting a car is advisable to explore the island's diverse landscapes.

Boca do Inferno Viewpoint Hotel (São Miguel)

One of the newest additions to São Miguel's luxury accommodations, this hotel offers unmatched views of the Sete Cidades crater and surrounding lakes.

- **Address:** Sete Cidades, São Miguel
- **Cost:** Nightly rates start at €300.
- **Features:** All rooms offer lake views, spa services, an infinity pool, a high-end restaurant, and exclusive access to several hiking trails.
- **Contact:** Contact details are available through major booking platforms.
- **How to Get There:** Located about 30 minutes from Ponta Delgada. As public transport options are limited, hiring a car is recommended.

Budget Stays: Hostels and Camping Options

Hostels

Hostels are ideal for travelers looking to save money without sacrificing the social aspect of traveling. They offer the opportunity to meet fellow travelers in communal settings.

The Nook Hostel (Ponta Delgada, São Miguel)

- **Address:** Rua de Lisboa, Ponta Delgada, São Miguel
- **Cost:** €20 per night for a dorm bed.
- **Features:** Offers a shared kitchen, lounge areas, free Wi-Fi, and includes breakfast. Private rooms are also available.
- **Contact:** +351 296 717 171
- **Getting There:** Located in the city center, about 7 km from João Paulo II Airport. A taxi or airport shuttle can get you there in about 10 minutes.

Pousada de Juventude (Angra do Heroísmo, Terceira)

- **Address:** Canada do Porto Judeu, Angra do Heroísmo, Terceira

- **Cost:** €15 to €25 per night, depending on the room type.
- **Features:** This hostel features both dormitory and private room options, a communal kitchen, and social areas.
- **Contact:** +351 295 212 522
- **Getting There:** The hostel is approximately 20 km from Lajes International Airport. Public buses and taxis are available for the transfer.

PJA - Pico Youth Hostel (Pico Island)

- **Address:** Caminho de Baixo, São Roque do Pico, Pico Island
- **Cost:** Dormitory beds start at €18 per night.
- **Features:** Facilities include a kitchen, dining area, free Wi-Fi, and bicycle rentals.
- **Contact:** +351 292 642 856
- **Getting There:** Located about 15 km from Pico Airport, accessible via taxi or pre-arranged shuttle services.

Camping Sites

For those who prefer to connect with nature, camping is a cost-effective way to experience the Azores' stunning natural landscapes.

Parque de Campismo das Sete Cidades (São Miguel)

- **Address:** Sete Cidades, São Miguel
- **Cost:** Approximately €5 per person per night.
- **Features:** Located near the beautiful Sete Cidades Lake, facilities include bathrooms, showers, a picnic area, and a small grocery store.
- **Contact:** +351 296 915 383
- **Getting There:** The camping site is about 30 km from Ponta Delgada. It

is best reached by car, and rental services are available in Ponta Delgada.

Camping Pico da Urze (Faial Island)

- **Address:** Rua da Praia, Almoxarife, Faial Island
- **Cost:** €4 per person per night for a tent site.
- **Features:** Offers stunning views of Mount Pico across the channel, with access to beaches and hiking trails.
- **Contact:** +351 292 943 636
- **Getting There:** Approximately 10 km from Horta Airport, accessible by taxi or local bus services.

Camping Santa Barbara (Terceira Island)

- **Address:** Estrada Regional, Santa Barbara, Terceira
- **Cost:** €6 per person per night.
- **Features:** Facilities include modern bathrooms, a snack bar, and direct beach access.
- **Contact:** +351 295 628 073
- **Getting There:** Around 20 km from Lajes Field Airport, with taxi and bus services available to the site.

Booking and Travel Tips

- **Reservations:** While reservations for hostels can be made online through platforms like Hostelworld or Booking.com, camping sites in the Azores are more relaxed, and booking in advance is not always necessary, except during peak summer months.
- **Pack Essentials:** For camping, ensure you have suitable gear such as a waterproof tent, a sleeping bag rated for cooler nights, and a portable stove if you plan to cook. Most camping sites offer basic supplies but bringing your own can save money.

- **Local Transport:** When staying in more remote locations or camping sites, consider renting a car as public transport may not cover all rural areas extensively.

Unique Stays: Agrotourism and Historical Properties

Agrotourism Estates
Quinta das Raiadas (São Miguel)

- **Overview:** Set on a working farm, this estate offers guests a chance to experience rural life in the Azores, including dairy farming and fruit cultivation.
- **Address:** Rua das Raiadas, Ponta Delgada, São Miguel
- **Cost:** Starting at €90 per night.
- **Features:** Guests can participate in daily farm activities, enjoy fresh organic meals prepared with ingredients from the farm, and explore the beautiful surroundings.
- **Contact:** +351 296 304 300
- **Getting There:** Approximately 15 km from João Paulo II Airport in Ponta Delgada. Car rental recommended for ease of access.

Casa do Pomar (Santa Maria)

- **Overview:** A charming farmhouse located in the lush hills of Santa Maria, offering beautiful views and a peaceful retreat.
- **Address:** Vila do Porto, Santa Maria
- **Cost:** €80 per night.
- **Features:** Features include horseback riding, a garden where guests can pick their own vegetables, and a traditional wood oven for bread baking.
- **Contact:** +351 292 242 500
- **Getting There:** About 10 km from Santa Maria Airport, with taxis and

pre-booked shuttles available for transfers.

Historical Properties
Solar do Conde (São Miguel)

- **Overview:** Built in the 17th century, this historic manor house is set in a botanical garden, offering a unique glimpse into the aristocratic past of the Azores.
- **Address:** Rua do Rosário, 36, São Miguel
- **Cost:** Rooms start at €110 per night.
- **Features:** The property includes elegantly furnished suites, an acclaimed restaurant serving local cuisine, and guided tours of the historic grounds.
- **Contact:** +351 296 629 431
- **Getting There:** Located in the town of Capelas, about 12 km from Ponta Delgada Airport. A taxi or rental car is advisable.

Quinta da Meia Eira (Faial)

- **Overview:** A seafront estate on Faial Island, dating back to the 19th century, now dedicated to sustainable tourism.
- **Address:** Rua da Meia Eira, Faial
- **Cost:** €95 per night for a double room.
- **Features:** The estate offers an organic breakfast, a natural swimming pool, and proximity to the shoreline for whale watching and other marine activities.
- **Contact:** +351 292 943 636
- **Getting There:** Approximately 8 km from Horta Airport. Shuttle services and car rentals are available.

Booking and Travel Tips

- **Advance Bookings:** Due to their unique nature and limited rooms, advance booking is highly recommended, especially during the peak season from June to August.
- **Check Seasonal Activities:** Many agrotourism estates offer seasonal activities such as grape harvesting or traditional cooking classes. Inquire about available activities when booking to enhance your stay.
- **Transportation:** Given the often rural and secluded locations of these properties, renting a car is usually the best way to ensure flexibility and ease of travel throughout your stay.
- **Explore Local Culture:** Use these stays as an opportunity to deeply explore the local culture and history. Engage with hosts and take part in offered activities for a full experience.

Dining and Cuisine

Culinary Delights

Staple Foods of the Azores

The diet in the Azores is largely influenced by the islands' geographical isolation and the resources available. Key staples include:

- **Seafood:** Given the islands' location in the Atlantic Ocean, seafood is a central component of the Azorean diet. Tuna, swordfish, and various types of shellfish are commonly consumed.
- **Dairy Products:** The lush, grassy landscapes provide ideal conditions for cattle, making dairy products like milk, cheese, and butter predominant in local cuisine.
- **Corn and Wheat:** These grains are staples for making breads and pastries, which are a must at any Azorean meal.
- **Yams and Sweet Potatoes:** Often used as side dishes, these root vegetables thrive in the volcanic soil of the islands.

Signature Dishes

Azorean dishes combine simplicity with rich flavors, often cooked slowly to enhance taste and tenderness.

Cozido das Furnas (São Miguel)

- A stew made by slow-cooking meats and vegetables in the ground, heated by volcanic steam. This method imparts a unique flavor that's quintessentially Azorean.
- **Where to Try:** Restaurante Tony's, Rua das Caldeiras, 56, 9675-042 Furnas, São Miguel. A meal costs around €20 per person.
- **Contact:** +351 296 584 256

Alcatra (Terceira)

- A rich beef or fish stew traditionally cooked in a clay pot. Seasoned with garlic, onions, and local spices, it's a heartwarming dish representative of Terceira's culinary heritage.
- **Where to Try:** Ti Choa, Rua de São Pedro, 18, 9700-187 Angra do Heroísmo, Terceira. Prices start at €15 per serving.
- **Contact:** +351 295 333 073

Queijadas da Graciosa

- Small, sweet pastries made from cheese, eggs, milk, and sugar. These treats are a specialty of Graciosa Island.
- **Where to Try:** Pastelaria Queijadas da Graciosa, Rua Mouzinho de Albuquerque, Santa Cruz da Graciosa. Each queijada costs about €1.
- **Contact:** +351 295 712 333

Culinary Traditions

Azorean culinary traditions are deeply rooted in community and family values, often associated with festivals and communal gatherings.

- **Espírito Santo Festivals:** These religious festivals are celebrated with elaborate feasts, where dishes like "Sopas do Espírito Santo" (a hearty broth made with bread, mint, and meat) are served to the community.
- **Family Gatherings:** Meals are typically multi-course affairs, starting

with soups, followed by seafood or meat dishes, and ending with desserts like "Bolo Lêvedo" (a sweet muffin).

Local Beverages

The Azores also boast a range of unique beverages, from wines to teas.

- **Wines:** Pico Island is renowned for its vineyards, producing distinctive wines due to its volcanic soil.
- **Where to Visit:** Cooperativa Vitivinícola da Ilha do Pico, Avenida Padre Nunes da Rosa, 29, Madalena, Pico. Wine tastings start at €5.
- **Contact:** +351 292 622 262
- **Tea:** The only tea plantations in Europe are found in São Miguel, offering aromatic and organic teas.
- **Where to Visit:** Gorreana Tea Factory, Maia, São Miguel. Free tours and tastings available.
- **Contact:** +351 296 442 349

Dining Etiquette

When dining in the Azores, it's customary to enjoy meals leisurely. Tipping is appreciated but not obligatory; around 10% of the bill is customary if you're satisfied with the service.

Restaurant Guide: From Fine Dining to Local Eateries

Fine Dining
Restaurante Atlântida (Ponta Delgada, São Miguel)

- **Overview:** Known for its sophisticated ambiance and creative dishes that showcase local seafood and produce.
- **Signature Dish:** Octopus lagareiro with sweet potato puree.

- **Address:** Rua Marquês da Praia e Monforte, 40, Ponta Delgada, São Miguel
- **Cost:** Approx. €50 per person for a three-course meal.
- **Contact:** +351 296 629 080
- **Getting There:** Located in the heart of Ponta Delgada, easily accessible by taxi or a short walk from most central hotels.

Anfiteatro Restaurant & Lounge (Ponta Delgada, São Miguel)

- **Overview:** A gastronomic delight that doubles as a culinary school during the day, offering innovative dishes in a modern setting.
- **Signature Dish:** Grilled limpets with Azorean garlic-butter sauce.
- **Address:** Largo de São Francisco, Ponta Delgada, São Miguel
- **Cost:** Around €45 per person.
- **Contact:** +351 296 308 340
- **Getting There:** Situated next to the Carlos Machado Museum, accessible by local bus lines or taxi.

Mid-Range Restaurants

O Corisco (Terceira)

- **Overview:** A cozy restaurant favored by locals for its authentic Azorean cuisine and friendly service.
- **Signature Dish:** Alcatra, a traditional pot roast that simmers for hours in a spicy wine sauce.
- **Address:** Rua da Sé 23, Angra do Heroísmo, Terceira
- **Cost:** Around €25 per person.
- **Contact:** +351 295 216 015
- **Getting There:** Centrally located in Angra do Heroísmo, it's an easy walk from the main city center attractions.

Casa Âncora (São Jorge)

- **Overview:** Praised for its fresh seafood and stunning views of the ocean.
- **Signature Dish:** Grilled bluefish with roasted vegetables.
- **Address:** Rua Cais da Calheta, São Jorge
- **Cost:** €30 per person.
- **Contact:** +351 295 416 424
- **Getting There:** Located on the southern coast of São Jorge, best reached by car or local taxis.

Local Eateries

Tasca das Tias (Pico)

- **Overview:** A charming eatery offering hearty, traditional meals in a rustic setting.
- **Signature Dish:** Espetada (beef skewers) with local yams.
- **Address:** Rua do Provedor 17, Madalena, Pico
- **Cost:** €15-€20 per person.
- **Contact:** +351 292 623 490
- **Getting There:** Located near the harbor of Madalena, easily reachable by foot from the town center.

Bar Caloura (São Miguel)

- **Overview:** Famous for its seafood dishes served right by the sea.
- **Signature Dish:** Fried chicharros (mackerel) with Azorean pepper sauce.
- **Address:** Baixa d'Areia, Caloura, São Miguel
- **Cost:** €20 per person.
- **Contact:** +351 296 913 283
- **Getting There:** Situated in the small coastal village of Caloura, accessible

by car or local bus services from Ponta Delgada.

Tips for Dining in the Azores

- **Reservations:** It's wise to book ahead, especially for dinner at popular restaurants.
- **Local Products:** Try to choose dishes featuring local ingredients like cheeses, sausages, and seafood for a true taste of Azorean flavors.
- **Meal Times:** Dinner in the Azores typically starts later than in many other places, often around 8 PM.
- **Dietary Needs:** Most restaurants are willing to accommodate dietary restrictions, but it's best to mention any specific requirements when booking.

Vegan and Vegetarian Options: Eating Green

Rotas da Ilha Verde (São Miguel)

- **Overview:** A pioneer in vegan and vegetarian cuisine in the Azores, Rotas da Ilha Verde offers a menu inspired by global flavors, made from locally sourced ingredients.
- **Signature Dishes:** Try the tofu scramble with sweet potato and the homemade vegan cheese.
- **Address:** Rua de Pedro Homem, 49, Ponta Delgada, São Miguel.
- **Cost:** Main dishes range from €9 to €15.
- **Contact:** +351 296 628 560
- **Getting There:** Located in the heart of Ponta Delgada, this restaurant is easily accessible on foot from downtown hotels or by local taxi services.

Terra Nostra Garden Restaurant (São Miguel)

- **Overview:** Situated within the Terra Nostra Garden Hotel, this restaurant offers a menu with several vegetarian options that utilize the rich geothermal resources of the Furnas Valley to create unique dishes.
- **Signature Dishes:** The "Cozido das Furnas" vegetarian version is a must-try.
- **Address:** Rua Padre José Jacinto Botelho, 5, Furnas, São Miguel.
- **Cost:** Vegetarian dishes start at €12.
- **Contact:** +351 296 549 090
- **Getting There:** The restaurant is about a 45-minute drive from Ponta Delgada, with car rental and taxi options available for transport.

Intz48 Coffee Roasters, Bar, and Vegan Bistro (Faial)

- **Overview:** Known for its excellent coffee and vegan-friendly menu, Intz48 is a modern bistro that focuses on sustainable, plant-based meals.
- **Signature Dishes:** The vegan burgers and wraps are local favorites.
- **Address:** Rua Conselheiro Medeiros, 48, Horta, Faial.
- **Cost:** Prices for main dishes are between €8 and €12.
- **Contact:** +351 292 292 392
- **Getting There:** Located in the center of Horta, it is easily reachable by foot from the city's main attractions and lodging.

Cantinho das Aromáticas (Terceira)

- **Overview:** This cozy eatery specializes in vegetarian and vegan dishes, incorporating aromatic herbs grown on their premises.
- **Signature Dishes:** Sample their seasonal soups and freshly made herbal teas.
- **Address:** Rua da Guarita, 50, Angra do Heroísmo, Terceira.
- **Cost:** An average meal costs around €10.
- **Contact:** +351 295 332 080
- **Getting There:** Situated in Angra do Heroísmo, it's a short walk from major historical sites and shopping areas.

Restaurante O Vegetariano (Pico)

- **Overview:** This restaurant offers a dedicated vegetarian and vegan menu that changes seasonally, based on what's locally available.
- **Signature Dishes:** The vegan açorda (bread stew) with wild mushrooms is highly recommended.
- **Address:** Rua do Mar, 13, Madalena, Pico.
- **Cost:** Expect to pay around €10 for a main dish.
- **Contact:** +351 292 623 490
- **Getting There:** Located in the town of Madalena, near the ferry terminal, making it a convenient stop for those traveling between islands.

Practical Tips for Dining

- **Reservations:** Particularly for dinner, it's wise to make reservations as these restaurants can be popular, especially during tourist season.
- **Local Produce:** Embrace the opportunity to try local fruits and vegetables; the Azores are known for their exceptional produce.
- **Ask for Specials:** Many restaurants have daily specials that are not always on the menu, often incorporating the freshest ingredients available.

Coffee Culture: Best Cafes and Teahouses

Louvre Michaelense (Ponta Delgada, São Miguel)

- **Overview:** This cafe is not only a favorite for its exceptional coffee but also for its historical setting and artisanal local products.
- **Signature Offerings:** Specialty coffees and a selection of local Azorean teas. Don't miss their homemade cakes and pastries.

- **Address:** Rua António José d'Almeida 8, Ponta Delgada, São Miguel
- **Cost:** Coffee prices start at €1.50, with pastries available from €2.00.
- **Contact:** +351 296 629 884
- **Getting There:** Located in the heart of Ponta Delgada, easily accessible by foot from the main shopping streets.

Café Central (Angra do Heroísmo, Terceira)

- **Overview:** Known for its vibrant atmosphere, Café Central is a popular meeting spot that blends traditional Azorean flavors with modern cafe culture.
- **Signature Offerings:** Excellent espresso, local pastries, and sandwiches. The afternoon tea service is highly recommended.
- **Address:** Praça Velha, Angra do Heroísmo, Terceira
- **Cost:** A cup of coffee costs around €1.20.
- **Contact:** +351 295 213 456
- **Getting There:** Centrally located in the historic center of Angra do Heroísmo, a short walk from the city's cathedral.

Fábrica de Chá Gorreana (São Miguel)

- **Overview:** As Europe's oldest and currently only tea plantation, Gorreana offers a unique experience. Visitors can enjoy freshly brewed teas directly from the source.
- **Signature Offerings:** Green and black teas harvested and processed on-site. Free tastings and tours of the tea plantation are available.
- **Address:** Plantações de Chá Gorreana, Maia, São Miguel
- **Cost:** Free entry; tea prices in the cafe start at €1.50.
- **Contact:** +351 296 442 349
- **Getting There:** Situated in the northern part of São Miguel, about 30 minutes drive from Ponta Delgada. Car rental or local tour buses can get you there.

O Conservatório (Ponta Delgada, São Miguel)

- **Overview:** This charming cafe and music venue offers a cozy atmosphere where visitors can enjoy coffee, tea, and live music performances.
- **Signature Offerings:** Specialty coffees and a variety of teas, alongside snacks and light meals. Their evening jazz sessions are a must-experience.
- **Address:** Rua de Lisboa 38, Ponta Delgada, São Miguel
- **Cost:** Expect to pay around €2 for a coffee.
- **Contact:** +351 296 288 408
- **Getting There:** Easily accessible by foot in Ponta Delgada's downtown area, near major hotels and tourist attractions.

Casa de Chá O Fio (Pico)

- **Overview:** Located in a picturesque setting, this teahouse is perfect for those looking to enjoy a quiet moment. They offer a wide range of Azorean and international teas.
- **Signature Offerings:** A selection of herbal and black teas, homemade cakes, and light meals.
- **Address:** Caminho de Baixo, São Roque do Pico, Pico
- **Cost:** Teas start at €2, with cakes and snacks from €3.
- **Contact:** +351 292 642 842
- **Getting There:** Cuddled in the rural area of São Roque, about a 15-minute drive from Pico Airport. Renting a car is advisable.

Adventures and Activities

Outdoor Thrills: Hiking, Cycling, and More

Hiking Trails

Sete Cidades Lake Trail (São Miguel)

- **Overview:** A scenic loop around the iconic twin lakes set in a massive volcanic crater, offering breathtaking views and lush vegetation.
- **Length:** Approximately 12 km (7.5 miles)
- **Difficulty:** Moderate
- **Location:** Sete Cidades, São Miguel
- **Starting Point:** Near the bridge in Sete Cidades village.
- **Cost:** Free
- **Contact for Guided Tours:** +351 296 288 081
- **Getting There:** Around 30 minutes drive from Ponta Delgada. Parking available at the trailhead.

Pico Mountain Trail (Pico Island)

- **Overview:** This trail leads to the summit of Mount Pico, Portugal's highest peak, providing a challenging hike with rewarding panoramic views.
- **Length:** 7.5 km (4.7 miles) one way

- **Difficulty:** Challenging
- **Location:** Mount Pico, Pico Island
- **Starting Point:** Mountain House (Casa da Montanha)
- **Cost:** €20 per person, including registration and a GPS tracker.
- **Contact:** +351 292 642 628
- **Getting There:** Accessible by car from Madalena, Pico. Parking available at Casa da Montanha.

Cycling Routes

East Coast Adventure Route (São Miguel)

- **Overview:** A popular cycling route that takes you along the picturesque eastern coast of São Miguel, featuring coastal views and stops at beaches and fishing villages.
- **Length:** 40 km (25 miles)
- **Difficulty:** Moderate
- **Location:** Starts at Nordeste, São Miguel
- **Cost:** Free, bike rentals available in Ponta Delgada for approximately €15 per day.
- **Contact for Bike Rentals:** +351 296 287 123
- **Getting There:** Nordeste is about 1 hour drive from Ponta Delgada.

Vineyard Trails (Pico Island)

- **Overview:** Cycle through UNESCO-listed vineyards, traditional villages, and along the rocky coastline. Ideal for experiencing local culture and scenic landscapes.
- **Length:** Variable, approximately 25 km (15.5 miles)
- **Difficulty:** Easy to moderate
- **Location:** Starts in Madalena, Pico Island

- **Cost:** Free, bike rentals available in Madalena for around €20 per day.
- **Contact for Bike Rentals:** +351 292 623 345
- **Getting There:** Accessible by foot or taxi from central Madalena.

Other Outdoor Sports

Surfing at Santa Bárbara Beach (São Miguel)

- **Overview:** Known for its consistent surf conditions, this beach is perfect for both beginners and experienced surfers.
- **Location:** Ribeira Grande, São Miguel
- **Cost:** Surfboard rentals and lessons start at €25 per session.
- **Contact for Surf School:** +351 296 470 000
- **Getting There:** 20 minutes drive from Ponta Delgada, with parking available near the beach.

Paragliding Over Green Hills (Faial)

- **Overview:** Take to the skies with a paragliding adventure that offers stunning aerial views of Faial's verdant landscapes and the surrounding sea.
- **Location:** Cabouco, Faial
- **Cost:** Tandem flights from €90 per person.
- **Contact for Paragliding Tours:** +351 292 943 676
- **Getting There:** 10 minutes drive from Horta; transport can be arranged by the paragliding company.

Marine Adventures: Scuba, Snorkeling, and Boat Tours

Scuba Diving

The Azores offer some of the best diving in the Atlantic, with clear waters and a rich marine ecosystem.

Besta Divers (São Miguel)

- **Overview:** Known for its professional service and excellent safety record, Besta Divers provides guided dives to some of the top spots around São Miguel.
- **Popular Dive Sites:** The Dori wreck and the Ambrosio reef are favorites, offering a chance to see manta rays and large schools of fish.
- **Address:** Rua Praia dos Santos, Ponta Delgada, São Miguel
- **Cost:** Dive packages start at €70, including gear rental.
- **Contact:** +351 296 285 123
- **Getting There:** Located in Ponta Delgada, just a 10-minute drive from the airport.

Pico Sport (Pico Island)

- **Overview:** Specializes in whale watching and diving trips, offering a unique combination of adventure sports.
- **Popular Dive Sites:** Princess Alice Bank, where divers can encounter pelagic fish and sometimes even sharks.
- **Address:** Rua João Bento Lima, Madalena, Pico
- **Cost:** Dive trips start at €90.
- **Contact:** +351 292 622 622
- **Getting There:** Situated in Madalena, the main town on Pico, easily reachable by taxi or bus from Pico Airport.

Snorkeling

For those who prefer snorkeling, the Azores' clear waters provide abundant opportunities to observe marine life in shallower waters.

Caloura Aquatic Paradise (São Miguel)

- **Overview:** Offers guided snorkeling tours in one of the most scenic spots on São Miguel, known for its clear waters and vibrant marine life.
- **Address:** Avenida da Caloura, Agua de Pau, São Miguel
- **Cost:** Snorkeling tours are around €45 per person.
- **Contact:** +351 296 916 787
- **Getting There:** About 20 minutes drive from Ponta Delgada; transportation can be arranged by the company.

Flores Dive Center (Flores)

- **Overview:** Located on the less touristy island of Flores, this center offers snorkeling trips that showcase untouched marine environments.
- **Address:** Rua do Emigrante, Santa Cruz das Flores, Flores
- **Cost:** Around €50 for a guided snorkeling session.
- **Contact:** +351 292 592 411
- **Getting There:** Accessible by a short drive from the Santa Cruz airport.

Boat Tours

Boat tours in the Azores can include whale watching, visits to remote islets, and even swimming with dolphins.

Futurismo Azores Adventures (São Miguel)

- **Overview:** One of the largest adventure companies in the Azores, offering comprehensive boat tours for whale watching and dolphin encounters.
- **Address:** Avenida João Bosco Mota Amaral, Ponta Delgada, São Miguel
- **Cost:** Whale watching tours start at €55 per person.
- **Contact:** +351 296 628 522
- **Getting There:** Located in the main marina of Ponta Delgada, easily reached by any city transport.

Faial Boat Tours (Faial)

- **Overview:** Specializes in customized tours around Faial and nearby islands, including Pico and São Jorge.
- **Address:** Rua Consul Dabney, Horta, Faial
- **Cost:** Custom tours start at €100 per person, depending on the duration and route.
- **Contact:** +351 292 391 616
- **Getting There:** Based in Horta's marina, a central location on Faial easily accessible on foot or by taxi.

Family Fun: Activities for All Ages

The Azores offer a treasure trove of activities suitable for families, providing both educational and fun experiences that cater to all ages. From interactive museums and engaging outdoor adventures to whale watching and beach days, these activities ensure memorable family vacations filled with discovery and excitement.

1. Terra Nostra Park (São Miguel)

- **Overview:** Known for its geothermal heated pools and extensive

botanical gardens, Terra Nostra Park is a fantastic spot for families to explore and relax.
- **Highlights:** The thermal pool is especially popular, providing a natural and warm bathing experience. The park also includes a maze, exotic plants from all over the world, and themed gardens.
- **Address:** Rua Padre José Jacinto Botelho, 5, Furnas, São Miguel
- **Cost:** €8 per adult, €4 for children under 10.
- **Contact:** +351 296 549 090
- **Getting There:** Located in Furnas, about a 45-minute drive from Ponta Delgada. Parking is available on-site.

2. Whale Watching Tours (Various Islands)

- **Overview:** The Azores are one of the world's premier destinations for whale watching, with opportunities to see sperm whales, dolphins, and occasionally blue whales.
- **Highlights:** Most tours offer educational components, teaching kids and adults about marine life and conservation efforts.
- **Providers:**
- Futurismo Azores Adventures, São Miguel: +351 296 628 522
- Picarus Sailing, Faial: +351 292 292 328
- **Cost:** Around €55 per adult, €35 per child.
- **Getting There:** Tours are available from major islands like São Miguel, Pico, and Faial, with easy access from local ports.

3. Lagoa das Furnas Monitoring & Research Centre (São Miguel)

- **Overview:** This center offers a hands-on learning experience about the geothermal activity of the Azores and its impact on local ecosystems.
- **Highlights:** Interactive exhibits and guided tours around the lake, showcasing bubbling springs and fumaroles.
- **Address:** Lagoa das Furnas, São Miguel
- **Cost:** €6 per adult, €2 for children.

- **Contact:** +351 296 584 256
- **Getting There:** Situated in the eastern part of São Miguel, approximately 30 minutes from Ponta Delgada by car.

4. Gruta do Carvão (São Miguel)

- **Overview:** The largest lava tube in São Miguel offers guided tours that are both educational and thrilling.
- **Highlights:** A safe adventure into the volcanic underground, suitable for kids and adults.
- **Address:** Rua do Paim, Ponta Delgada, São Miguel
- **Cost:** €8 per adult, €4 per child.
- **Contact:** +351 296 284 155
- **Getting There:** Located in Ponta Delgada, easily accessible by car or public transport from the city center.

5. Praia de Santa Bárbara (São Miguel)

- **Overview:** A sandy beach known for its gentle waves and wide shores, ideal for families looking to enjoy a day at the beach.
- **Highlights:** Surf schools offer lessons for all ages, making it a great spot for beginners.
- **Address:** Ribeira Grande, São Miguel
- **Cost:** Free access; surf lessons start at about €35 per person.
- **Contact for Surf School:** +351 296 636 505
- **Getting There:** 10 minutes from Ribeira Grande by car. Public parking is available nearby.

6. Monte Palace Tropical Garden (São Miguel)

- **Overview:** A breathtaking garden with themes from different parts of the world, featuring koi ponds, sculptures, and themed sections.
- **Highlights:** The Children's area with interactive games and the Japanese

garden.

- **Address:** Monte Palace, São Miguel
- **Cost:** €10 per adult, free for children under 15.
- **Contact:** +351 296 205 500
- **Getting There:** About 20 minutes drive from Ponta Delgada. Parking available on-site.

The Arts: Galleries, Theatres, and Cultural Spaces

Galleries

Arquipélago – Contemporary Arts Center (Ribeira Grande, São Miguel)

- **Overview:** A major hub for contemporary art in the Azores, hosting exhibitions, workshops, and performances from local and international artists.
- **Address:** Rua Adolfo Coutinho de Medeiros, Ribeira Grande, São Miguel
- **Exhibitions:** Features both permanent and temporary exhibitions, often focusing on themes relevant to island life and global environmental issues.
- **Cost:** Free admission to most exhibitions.
- **Contact:** +351 296 470 130
- **Getting There:** Located in the northern part of São Miguel, about 20 minutes drive from Ponta Delgada. Public transport and parking are available.

Fábrica da Baleia de Porto Pim (Faial)

- **Overview:** This gallery and museum are set in a restored whale processing factory, offering insights into the historical and cultural

THE AZORES TRAVEL GUIDE 2025

significance of whaling in the Azores.

- **Address:** Estrada de Porto Pim, Faial
- **Cost:** €2 for adults, free for children under 12.
- **Contact:** +351 292 292 140
- **Getting There:** Situated in the bay of Porto Pim, easily accessible from the center of Horta by foot or by car.

Theatres

Teatro Micaelense (Ponta Delgada, São Miguel)

- **Overview:** The main cultural venue on São Miguel for performing arts, including music, dance, and theatre.
- **Address:** Largo de São João, Ponta Delgada, São Miguel
- **Performances:** Hosts a range of performances from classical concerts to modern dance and theatrical plays.
- **Cost:** Ticket prices vary depending on the event, generally ranging from €10 to €50.
- **Contact:** +351 296 308 340
- **Getting There:** Centrally located in Ponta Delgada, within walking distance from many hotels and restaurants.

Coliseu Micaelense (Ponta Delgada, São Miguel)

- **Overview:** Another key venue for larger scale performances and events, including concerts, festivals, and special cultural events.
- **Address:** Rua de Lisboa, Ponta Delgada, São Miguel
- **Cost:** Prices vary based on the event, with some free community events.
- **Contact:** +351 296 209 500
- **Getting There:** Also located in Ponta Delgada, it is adjacent to major city attractions and easily reachable by public transportation.

Cultural Spaces

Biblioteca Pública e Arquivo Regional de Ponta Delgada (São Miguel)

- **Overview:** More than just a library, this venue hosts readings, small concerts, and exhibitions, making it a vital part of São Miguel's cultural scene.
- **Address:** Rua José do Canto, 1, Ponta Delgada, São Miguel
- **Cost:** Free access to most events.
- **Contact:** +351 296 304 400
- **Getting There:** Located in the historic center of Ponta Delgada, accessible on foot or by local bus.

Casa dos Açores (Terceira)

- **Overview:** Cultural center dedicated to promoting Azorean culture and arts, including music, crafts, and literature.
- **Address:** Rua da Sé, Angra do Heroísmo, Terceira
- **Cost:** Free entry; workshop prices may vary.
- **Contact:** +351 295 217 845
- **Getting There:** Situated in the heart of Angra do Heroísmo, a short walk from central landmarks and parking areas.

After Dark: Nightlife and Entertainment

Nightlife Hotspots: Where to Party

The nightlife in the Azores might not rival the world's biggest party capitals, but it offers a charming and vibrant scene suited to those looking to unwind after dark. From laid-back bars with live local music to energetic nightclubs where you can dance until the early hours, here's where you can enjoy the best of the Azorean nightlife.

Bars and Pubs
Bar Caloura (São Miguel)

- **Overview:** Crouched by the sea, Bar Caloura combines breathtaking views with a relaxed atmosphere, making it perfect for a sunset drink.
- **Signature Drinks:** Try the local passion fruit poncha.
- **Address:** Rua do Jubileu, Caloura, São Miguel
- **Cost:** Cocktails start at €5.
- **Contact:** +351 296 912 334
- **Getting There:** About 20 minutes drive from Ponta Delgada. It's recommended to drive or take a taxi due to limited public transport in the evening.

Peter Café Sport (Faial)

- **Overview:** An iconic sailor's bar known globally among yachting communities, offering a lively atmosphere filled with maritime memorabilia.
- **Signature Drinks:** The gin and tonic are famous here, made with the bar's own brand of gin.
- **Address:** Rua José Azevedo "Peter," Horta, Faial
- **Cost:** Drinks start at around €4.
- **Contact:** +351 292 292 327
- **Getting There:** Located in the heart of Horta's marina, it's easily accessible on foot from the port area.

Clubs
Clube Naval (Pico)

- **Overview:** A popular spot among locals and tourists alike, Clube Naval is the go-to place in Pico for late-night dancing and themed party nights.
- **Address:** Rua dos Biscoitos, Pico
- **Cost:** Entry usually free; drinks priced around €5.
- **Contact:** +351 292 629 730
- **Getting There:** Situated near the main town of Madalena, it is accessible by taxi or a short walk from nearby accommodations.

Kafka Bar (São Miguel)

- **Overview:** Known for its vibrant atmosphere and eclectic music selection, from live bands playing traditional Portuguese music to DJs spinning contemporary hits.
- **Address:** Avenida Roberto Ivens, Ponta Delgada, São Miguel
- **Cost:** Free entry, with drinks starting at €4.
- **Contact:** +351 296 628 200
- **Getting There:** Located in downtown Ponta Delgada, within walking distance from most city center hotels.

Live Music Venues

Coliseu Micaelense (São Miguel)

- **Overview:** The primary concert venue in São Miguel hosting various performances, from local folk bands to international acts.
- **Address:** Rua de Lisboa, Ponta Delgada, São Miguel
- **Cost:** Ticket prices vary depending on the event, usually starting at €10.
- **Contact:** +351 296 209 500
- **Getting There:** Centrally located in Ponta Delgada, easy to reach by public transport or taxi.

Ramada dos Biscoitos (Terceira)

- **Overview:** This venue offers a rustic and authentic Azorean entertainment experience with regular live music nights that showcase traditional dances and songs.
- **Address:** Canada do Martelo, 24, Praia da Vitória, Terceira
- **Cost:** Generally free entry; drinks and snacks are reasonably priced.
- **Contact:** +351 295 908 300
- **Getting There:** Situated in the countryside of Terceira, about a 15-minute drive from Angra do Heroísmo. Best accessed by car.

Cultural Nights: Music and Dance

Traditional Folk Performances

Grupo Folclórico de Santa Cruz (Santa Cruz, Flores)

- **Overview:** This folk group performs traditional Azorean dances and music, showcasing the unique cultural blend of Portuguese and local influences.
- **Performance Nights:** Typically held on Friday nights during the

summer months.

- **Address:** Largo de São Boaventura, Santa Cruz das Flores, Flores.
- **Cost:** Free entry; donations are appreciated.
- **Contact:** +351 292 590 400
- **Getting There:** Located in the town center of Santa Cruz, accessible by foot from most parts of town.

Casa do Trabalhador (São Miguel)

- **Overview:** Offers regular evening performances featuring traditional music and dance from São Miguel.
- **Performance Nights:** Most Saturday evenings throughout the year.
- **Address:** Rua do Mercado, Ponta Delgada, São Miguel.
- **Cost:** Around €5 per person.
- **Contact:** +351 296 287 206
- **Getting There:** Centrally located in Ponta Delgada, easy to reach by local bus or taxi.

Contemporary Music and Festivals
Angra Jazz Festival (Terceira)

- **Overview:** An annual event that brings together local and international jazz artists in Angra do Heroísmo.
- **Event Month:** Usually held in October.
- **Address:** Centro Cultural e de Congressos, Angra do Heroísmo, Terceira.
- **Cost:** Ticket prices vary, typically around €20 for a day pass.
- **Contact:** +351 295 401 700
- **Getting There:** The venue is in the city center, easily accessible by local transport.

Monte Verde Festival (São Miguel)

- **Overview:** A popular music festival featuring a mix of genres, from rock and pop to electronic. It draws a young crowd and features both local bands and international acts.
- **Event Month:** August
- **Address:** Ribeira Grande, São Miguel.
- **Cost:** Tickets start at €30 for a single day.
- **Contact:** +351 296 470 000
- **Getting There:** Ribeira Grande is about 15 minutes drive from Ponta Delgada. Shuttle services are often available from major points on the island during the festival.

Dance Clubs Featuring Traditional and Modern Dance
Clube Naval (Pico)

- **Overview:** Though primarily a nightlife spot, Clube Naval also hosts special dance nights where traditional Portuguese dances are taught and practiced.
- **Address:** Rua dos Biscoitos, Pico.
- **Cost:** Free entry on dance nights; drinks at bar prices.
- **Contact:** +351 292 629 730
- **Getting There:** Located near the harbor of Madalena, it's easily accessible by foot or local taxi.

Teatro Micaelense (São Miguel)

- **Overview:** While primarily a theatre, it also hosts dance performances and workshops, including traditional dances.
- **Address:** Largo de São João, Ponta Delgada, São Miguel.
- **Cost:** Varies by event, generally around €10 for performances.
- **Contact:** +351 296 308 340
- **Getting There:** In the heart of Ponta Delgada, accessible by local transport.

Quiet Corners: Evening Relaxation Spots

For those seeking a peaceful retreat from the day's adventures, the Azores offer several serene spots perfect for a relaxed evening. From cozy cafés and tranquil gardens to beachfront locales, these venues provide a calm atmosphere where you can unwind and enjoy the slower pace of island life.

Cafés and Tea Houses
O Chá da Barca (Pico Island)

- **Overview:** A charming tea house overlooking the Atlantic, known for its wide selection of teas and quiet ambiance.
- **Signature Offerings:** Azorean green and black teas, homemade cakes.
- **Address:** Avenida do Mar, Madalena, Pico.
- **Cost:** Teas and coffees from €1.50, cakes around €3.
- **Contact:** +351 292 623 344
- **Getting There:** Located along the main coastal road in Madalena, accessible by car or local bus.

Café Garajau (Terceira)

- **Overview:** Situated in Angra do Heroísmo, this café offers a cozy spot for an evening coffee or tea, with a small library corner perfect for reading.
- **Signature Offerings:** Specialty coffees, herbal teas, light snacks.
- **Address:** Rua da Sé, Angra do Heroísmo, Terceira.
- **Cost:** Coffee and tea from €2.
- **Contact:** +351 295 217 845
- **Getting There:** Centrally located in the historical center, easily reachable on foot from nearby hotels and attractions.

Gardens and Parks

Jardim José do Canto (São Miguel)

- **Overview:** A historic botanical garden in Ponta Delgada, offering a tranquil setting with lush greenery and a small lake.
- **Address:** Rua José do Canto, Ponta Delgada, São Miguel.
- **Cost:** Entry fee is €2.
- **Contact:** +351 296 629 431
- **Getting There:** In the eastern part of Ponta Delgada, within walking distance from the city center.

Parque Terra Nostra (São Miguel)

- **Overview:** Famous for its thermal pool and extensive gardens, it's an ideal spot for a soothing evening stroll.
- **Address:** Rua Padre José Jacinto Botelho, Furnas, São Miguel.
- **Cost:** €8, includes access to the thermal pool.
- **Contact:** +351 296 549 090
- **Getting There:** Located in Furnas, about a 40-minute drive from Ponta Delgada.

Beachfront Walks
Praia do Populo (São Miguel)

- **Overview:** A long sandy beach with a boardwalk, perfect for an evening walk, watching the sunset over the ocean.
- **Address:** Largo da Praia do Populo, São Miguel.
- **Cost:** Free access.
- **Getting There:** About 10 minutes drive from Ponta Delgada; parking available near the beach.

Praia da Vitória (Terceira)

- **Overview:** A vibrant beach promenade with cafes and a relaxed atmosphere, ideal for winding down after a busy day.
- **Address:** Avenida Beira Mar, Praia da Vitória, Terceira.
- **Cost:** Free access to the promenade; café prices vary.
- **Getting There:** Located in the heart of Praia da Vitória, easily accessible on foot from the town center.

Cultural Venues
Biblioteca Pública e Arquivo Regional de Ponta Delgada (São Miguel)

- **Overview:** Not just a library, this venue often hosts quiet evening events like book readings or small acoustic concerts.
- **Address:** Rua José do Canto, 1, Ponta Delgada, São Miguel.
- **Cost:** Most events are free; occasionally, there might be a small charge for special performances.
- **Contact:** +351 296 304 400
- **Getting There:** Situated in the center of Ponta Delgada, accessible by public transport.

Shopping and Commerce

Shopping Locales: Where to Buy Local and Luxe

Local Crafts and Specialty Shops

Cerâmica Vieira (Lagoa, São Miguel)

- **Overview:** A ceramic factory and shop renowned for its traditional Azorean pottery, featuring intricate designs inspired by local culture.
- **Products:** Hand-painted tiles, ceramic dishes, decorative pieces.
- **Address:** Rua de São Francisco 2, Lagoa, São Miguel.
- **Cost:** Prices start at €10 for small items and can go up to several hundred for elaborate pieces.
- **Contact:** +351 296 912 511
- **Getting There:** Located in Lagoa, approximately 10 minutes by car from Ponta Delgada. Parking is available on-site.

Mercado da Graça (Ponta Delgada, São Miguel)

- **Overview:** The main market in Ponta Delgada offering a wide range of local products including fresh produce, flowers, fish, and cheeses.
- **Products:** Local cheeses, pineapples, passion fruit, various handicrafts.
- **Address:** Rua do Mercado, Ponta Delgada, São Miguel.
- **Cost:** Entry is free; products are reasonably priced.

- **Contact:** +351 296 287 342
- **Getting There:** Centrally located in Ponta Delgada, easily accessible on foot from downtown hotels.

Luxury Goods and Fashion Boutiques

Angra Shopping (Terceira)

- **Overview:** The premier shopping center in Terceira, featuring a range of local and international brands, including luxury goods.
- **Products:** High-end fashion, jewelry, electronics, and more.
- **Address:** Rua de São João, Angra do Heroísmo, Terceira.
- **Cost:** Prices vary widely depending on the store and product.
- **Contact:** +351 295 204 020
- **Getting There:** Located in the heart of Angra do Heroísmo, it's within walking distance from the city center and has ample parking.

La Vie Funchal Shopping Center (São Miguel)

- **Overview:** A modern shopping mall with a mix of local boutiques and international luxury brands.
- **Products:** Designer clothes and accessories, perfumes, gourmet foods.
- **Address:** Avenida Doutor João Bosco Mota Amaral, Ponta Delgada, São Miguel.
- **Cost:** Premium pricing for luxury brands.
- **Contact:** +351 296 630 000
- **Getting There:** Located in Ponta Delgada, accessible by local bus routes and taxis, with dedicated parking.

Artisan Markets and Fairs

Feira de Artesanato (São Miguel)

- **Overview:** A periodic artisan fair that showcases local craftspeople and artists from across São Miguel.
- **Products:** Handmade jewelry, woven baskets, embroidered linens, and homemade food products.
- **Address:** Rotates locations within São Miguel; often held in public squares or event halls.
- **Cost:** Entry is typically free; prices for goods are moderate.
- **Contact:** Check local event listings for dates and locations.
- **Getting There:** Event locations are usually central and well-served by public transportation.

Espaço Azores (Pico)

- **Overview:** A boutique that brings together high-quality crafts and products from across the Azores.
- **Products:** Azorean tea, lava stone jewelry, locally produced wine.
- **Address:** Rua do Provedor, Madalena, Pico.
- **Cost:** Mid-range to high, depending on the product.
- **Contact:** +351 292 623 345
- **Getting There:** Located in the town of Madalena, it's easy to reach on foot from the main tourist areas, with nearby parking available.

Crafts and Souvenirs

Ceramics and Pottery

Cerâmica Vieira (Lagoa, São Miguel)

- **Overview:** A family-run pottery workshop known for its distinctive blue and white ceramics, inspired by the ocean and sky of the Azores.
- **Products:** Decorative and functional ceramics including dishes, vases, and tiles.
- **Address:** Rua de São Francisco 2, Lagoa, São Miguel.
- **Cost:** Prices range from €10 for small decorative items to over €100 for elaborate pieces.
- **Contact:** +351 296 912 511
- **Getting There:** Located in Lagoa, about 10 minutes drive from Ponta Delgada. Ample parking is available.

Textiles and Linens

Fábrica de Lã de São Jorge (São Jorge)

- **Overview:** This mill produces high-quality woolen goods using traditional methods and local wool.
- **Products:** Woolen sweaters, scarves, and blankets.
- **Address:** Rua do Parque, Velas, São Jorge.
- **Cost:** Sweaters start at €50, scarves at €20.
- **Contact:** +351 295 432 323
- **Getting There:** Situated in Velas, accessible by car or local bus services from around the island.

Food and Drink

Gorreana Tea Plantation (São Miguel)

- **Overview:** The oldest and only tea plantation in Europe offers a range of organic teas grown on the island.
- **Products:** Green and black teas.
- **Address:** Plantações de Chá Gorreana, Maia, São Miguel.
- **Cost:** Around €5 for a standard pack of tea.
- **Contact:** +351 296 442 349
- **Getting There:** Located in the northern part of São Miguel, about 30 minutes drive from Ponta Delgada. Parking is available on-site.

Queijaria Artesanal (Pico)

- **Overview:** A cheese shop specializing in artisanal cheeses made from local cow's milk.
- **Products:** Variety of cheeses including the famous "Queijo do Pico."
- **Address:** Rua dos Biscoitos, Pico.
- **Cost:** Prices start at €6 for a small cheese.
- **Contact:** +351 292 623 345
- **Getting There:** Located in Madalena, easy to reach by car or local bus from anywhere on Pico.

Arts and Crafts

Azores Handicraft (Terceira)

- **Overview:** Shop offering a wide selection of handcrafted goods made by local artisans.
- **Products:** Handmade jewelry, embroidered linens, wicker baskets, and

hand-painted figurines.
- **Address:** Rua de São João, Angra do Heroísmo, Terceira.
- **Cost:** Jewelry from €15, linens from €10.
- **Contact:** +351 295 217 845
- **Getting There:** Centrally located in Angra do Heroísmo, accessible on foot or by taxi.

Unique Souvenirs
Lava Rock Carvings (São Miguel)

- **Overview:** Local artisans carve the volcanic rock of the islands into beautiful sculptures and jewelry.
- **Products:** Sculptures, necklaces, and other decorative items made from basalt.
- **Address:** Local craft markets and shops across São Miguel.
- **Cost:** Starting at €20 for small carvings.
- **Contact:** Look for artisans at local markets or inquire at tourist information centers.
- **Getting There:** Available at most tourist-heavy locations and craft markets throughout São Miguel.

Market Days: Schedule and What to Expect

São Miguel - Mercado da Graça, Ponta Delgada

- **Overview:** The primary market in São Miguel, offering a wide array of local products from fresh produce to crafts.
- **Schedule:** Open daily from 7:00 AM to 7:00 PM, with Saturdays being the busiest and most vibrant.
- **Products:** Fresh fruits, vegetables, flowers, local cheeses, fish, and

handmade crafts.
- **Address:** Rua do Mercado, Ponta Delgada, São Miguel.
- **Getting There:** Located in the heart of Ponta Delgada, easily accessible on foot from downtown hotels or by local bus.
- **Contact:** +351 296 287 342

Terceira - Angra do Heroísmo Municipal Market

- **Overview:** Known for its lively atmosphere and quality local products, this market encapsulates the spirit of Terceira.
- **Schedule:** Monday to Saturday from 8:00 AM to 6:00 PM.
- **Products:** Specialty sausages, dairy products, handicrafts, and seasonal fruits and vegetables.
- **Address:** Rua de São João, Angra do Heroísmo, Terceira.
- **Getting There:** Centrally located, it's a short walk from most parts of the city center. Public parking is available nearby.
- **Contact:** +351 295 401 700

Faial - Horta Farmers' Market
- **Overview:** A smaller but equally charming market, focusing on organic and locally sourced produce.
- **Schedule:** Saturdays from 8:00 AM to 1:00 PM.
- **Products:** Organic vegetables, homemade bread, jams, and artisanal cheese.
- **Address:** Largo Duque d'Ávila e Bolama, Horta, Faial.
- **Getting There:** Situated in the center of Horta, accessible by foot or local taxi.
- **Contact:** +351 292 292 327

Pico - Madalena Market

- **Overview:** A bustling market known for Pico wine and a variety of seafood.
- **Schedule:** Every Friday from early morning until around 2:00 PM.
- **Products:** Fresh fish, Pico wine, handicrafts, and baked goods.
- **Address:** Rua Cardeal Costa Nunes, Madalena, Pico.
- **Getting There:** Located near the main harbor area, easy to reach on foot from the ferry terminal and nearby accommodations.
- **Contact:** +351 292 623 345

São Jorge - Velas Market

- **Overview:** Celebrated for its local cheeses and handmade crafts, this market reflects the agricultural strength of São Jorge.
- **Schedule:** Wednesday and Saturday mornings from 7:00 AM to 12:00 PM.
- **Products:** São Jorge cheese, handcrafted pottery, and fresh produce.
- **Address:** Mercado Municipal de Velas, São Jorge.
- **Getting There:** In the town of Velas, this market is a short walk from the main town area. Local bus services are available for those coming from farther away.
- **Contact:** +351 295 430 000

Tips for Market Shopping

- **Arrive Early:** The best products tend to sell out quickly, so arriving early ensures you get the freshest items.
- **Cash is King:** While some vendors may accept credit cards, cash is preferred and sometimes the only option.

- **Local Interaction:** Don't hesitate to strike up conversations with vendors. Many are proud of their offerings and can provide insights into the best ways to enjoy their products.
- **Sustainable Shopping:** Bring your own bags to reduce plastic use, supporting the Azores' environmental efforts.

Beaches and Coastal Retreats

Top Beach Picks: Sun, Sand, and Surf

Sunbathing

Praia de Santa Bárbara (São Miguel)

- **Overview:** Known for its expansive black sand and stunning backdrop of mountains, it's perfect for sunbathers looking for spacious relaxation spots.
- **Address:** Ribeira Grande, São Miguel.
- **Facilities:** Lifeguards, showers, changing rooms, and a beach bar.
- **Getting There:** Located on the north coast of São Miguel, about 10 minutes drive from Ribeira Grande. Parking available near the beach.
- **Contact:** +351 296 470 000

Praia do Almoxarife (Faial)

- **Overview:** A beautiful black sand beach with clear views of Pico Mountain across the channel, ideal for peaceful sunbathing.
- **Address:** Almoxarife, Faial.
- **Facilities:** Includes lifeguards during the summer, beachside café, and picnic areas.
- **Getting There:** Just a few kilometers north of Horta, accessible by car

or local bus services with parking available onsite.

- **Contact:** +351 292 208 200

Swimming

Praia Formosa (Santa Maria)

- **Overview:** This white sand beach is one of the few in the Azores and is renowned for its calm, turquoise waters, making it ideal for swimming.
- **Address:** Praia Formosa, Santa Maria.
- **Facilities:** Lifeguards in summer, beach bars, and restaurants nearby.
- **Getting There:** About 10 minutes drive from Vila do Porto. Ample parking is available.
- **Contact:** +351 296 820 000

Praia do Porto Pim (Faial)

- **Overview:** Enclosed by high cliffs, its sheltered waters are warm and tranquil, perfect for families and swimmers.
- **Address:** Porto Pim, Faial.
- **Facilities:** Lifeguards, cafes, and historical attractions nearby.
- **Getting There:** Short walk from the town of Horta, with parking areas close by.
- **Contact:** +351 292 392 327

Surfing

Praia do Norte (Faial)

- **Overview:** Favoured by surfers for its consistent waves and less crowded conditions compared to more popular spots.
- **Address:** Praia do Norte, Faial.
- **Facilities:** Limited; best for experienced surfers bringing their own equipment.
- **Getting There:** About 20 minutes drive from Horta. Limited parking available.
- **Contact:** Local surf shops in Horta for more information.

Praia de Santa Bárbara (São Miguel)

- **Overview:** A hotspot for surfing in the Azores, hosting international surfing competitions thanks to its powerful and consistent waves.
- **Address:** Ribeira Grande, São Miguel.
- **Facilities:** Surf schools, rentals, lifeguards, and beach bars.
- **Getting There:** Accessible by car from Ribeira Grande with ample parking.
- **Contact:** +351 296 470 000; numerous surf schools offer lessons and equipment rental.

Coastal Walks: Best Routes

The Azores, with their dramatic coastlines and stunning ocean views, offer some of the best coastal walking routes in the world. These walks not only provide breathtaking vistas but also an opportunity to experience the unique geological and botanical features of the islands.

São Miguel: Sete Cidades Coastal Loop

- **Overview:** This route circles the rim of the massive Sete Cidades caldera, offering panoramic views of both the twin lakes and the Atlantic Ocean.
- **Distance:** Approximately 12 kilometers.
- **Difficulty:** Moderate, with some steep sections.
- **Starting Point:** Lagoa Azul lookout, accessible from Ponta Delgada via the EN9-1A.
- **Highlights:** Viewpoints over Lagoa Azul and Lagoa Verde, lush endemic flora, and the abandoned Monte Palace Hotel.
- **Facilities:** Limited on the route; several small cafes and facilities available in Sete Cidades village.
- **Getting There:** Around 30 minutes drive from Ponta Delgada. Parking available at the starting point.
- **Contact:** São Miguel tourism office at +351 296 205 760 for guided tour options.

Faial: Capelinhos Volcano to Morro de Castelo Branco

- **Overview:** This walk takes you along the western coast of Faial, through the haunting landscape of the Capelinhos volcano, and ends at the striking white cliffs of Morro de Castelo Branco.
- **Distance:** 16 kilometers.
- **Difficulty:** Moderate to challenging, primarily due to length and exposure to elements.
- **Starting Point:** Capelinhos Volcano Visitor Center.
- **Highlights:** The Capelinhos volcano, lunar landscapes, views of the neighboring islands on clear days.
- **Facilities:** Visitor center at the start has amenities; otherwise, limited until Morro de Castelo Branco.
- **Getting There:** Capelinhos is about 40 minutes drive from Horta. Public transport is sparse, so a taxi or rental car is recommended.

- **Contact:** Faial tourism office at +351 292 292 237.

Pico: São Roque to Cachorro

- **Overview:** A scenic coastal trail that offers views of Pico's dramatic lava rock coastline and passes through quaint fishing villages.
- **Distance:** 8 kilometers.
- **Difficulty:** Easy to moderate, with mostly flat terrain but some rough patches.
- **Starting Point:** São Roque do Pico.
- **Highlights:** Natural swimming pools, vineyards classified by UNESCO as World Heritage, and traditional Açorean whaling boats.
- **Facilities:** Restaurants and cafes in São Roque and Cachorro.
- **Getting There:** São Roque is accessible by road from Madalena, about 20 minutes drive. Parking available in São Roque.
- **Contact:** Pico tourism office at +351 292 642 444.

Terceira: Serra do Cume to Praia da Vitória

- **Overview:** This route starts at the panoramic viewpoint of Serra do Cume, descending to the beautiful beach town of Praia da Vitória.
- **Distance:** About 10 kilometers.
- **Difficulty:** Moderate, descending from high elevation.
- **Starting Point:** Serra do Cume viewpoint.
- **Highlights:** Panoramic views of patchwork fields, Praia da Vitória bay.
- **Facilities:** Full amenities available in Praia da Vitória.
- **Getting There:** Serra do Cume is about 15 minutes drive from Angra do Heroísmo. Public buses or taxis can be used to return from Praia da Vitória.
- **Contact:** Terceira tourism office at +351 295 403 800.

Waterfront Dining: Must-Visit Locations

São Miguel: Restaurante São Pedro

- **Overview:** This upscale restaurant in Ponta Delgada offers a refined dining experience with panoramic views of the Atlantic Ocean.
- **Cuisine:** Specializes in seafood dishes that incorporate fresh, local ingredients.
- **Address:** Avenida Infante Dom Henrique, Ponta Delgada, São Miguel.
- **Price Range:** €30 - €50 per person.
- **Specialties:** The grilled limpets and tuna steak are highly recommended.
- **Contact:** +351 296 282 677
- **Getting There:** Located along the main coastal promenade in Ponta Delgada, easily accessible by taxi or a short walk from the city center.
- **Features:** Outdoor seating available; reservations are advised, especially during sunset hours.

Terceira: Beira Mar São Mateus

- **Overview:** Known for its delightful seafood and rustic charm, this restaurant is situated in a small fishing village, offering authentic Azorean dining by the water.
- **Cuisine:** Focuses on traditional Azorean seafood.
- **Address:** Rua Beira Mar, São Mateus, Terceira.
- **Price Range:** €25 - €40 per person.
- **Specialties:** Octopus stew and the fresh catch of the day.
- **Contact:** +351 295 642 392
- **Getting There:** Approximately 10 minutes drive from Angra do Heroísmo. Parking is available on-site.
- **Features:** The terrace overlooks the fishing port, providing a genuine seaside experience.

Faial: Restaurante Genuíno

- **Overview:** Owned by a renowned Azorean sailor, Genuíno Madruga, this restaurant in Horta offers a direct view of the marina and specializes in dishes that reflect the island's maritime heritage.
- **Cuisine:** Features a mix of international and local dishes with an emphasis on fresh, local seafood.
- **Address:** Rua de São Salvador, Horta, Faial.
- **Price Range:** €20 - €35 per person.
- **Specialties:** Scallops wrapped in bacon and the seafood rice.
- **Contact:** +351 292 292 327
- **Getting There:** Situated close to the Horta Marina, within walking distance from the ferry terminal.
- **Features:** Outdoor seating is available with views of the marina where yachts from around the world anchor.

Pico: Cella Bar

- **Overview:** This award-winning bar and restaurant boasts a modern architectural design and offers spectacular views of the Atlantic and the neighboring island of Faial.
- **Cuisine:** Modern fusion cuisine, with a focus on innovative seafood dishes.
- **Address:** Estrada Regional, Madalena, Pico.
- **Price Range:** €30 - €45 per person.
- **Specialties:** Black sausage with pineapple and local wine pairings.
- **Contact:** +351 292 623 490
- **Getting There:** Located on the western coast of Pico, near Madalena. It's best accessed by car, with parking available on-site.
- **Features:** The building itself is a tourist attraction, offering multi-level terraces overlooking the sea.

São Jorge: Fornos de Lava

- **Overview:** Nested in an old stone building, this restaurant in São Jorge specializes in local cuisine cooked in wood ovens, providing diners with a rustic yet charming dining experience by the sea.
- **Cuisine:** Traditional Azorean dishes, many cooked in a wood-fired oven.
- **Address:** Canada do Porto, Velas, São Jorge.
- **Price Range:** €20 - €35 per person.
- **Specialties:** Alcatra (beef pot roast) and limpets.
- **Contact:** +351 295 412 333
- **Getting There:** A few minutes drive from the center of Velas, with signs directing to the restaurant along the main road.
- **Features:** Offers seating close to the water's edge, providing an immersive seaside atmosphere.

Practical Tips and Advice

Communication: Phones, Internet, and Media

Mobile Phones and Service Providers

The Azores have good mobile network coverage, with services provided by three main operators: MEO, Vodafone, and NOS. Coverage is generally strong in urban areas and tourist spots but can be patchy in remote or mountainous areas.

MEO

- **Overview:** Offers extensive coverage across all islands and various data packages tailored to tourists.
- **Tourist SIM Cards:** Available at MEO stores and kiosks at airports. Packages start at around €15 for 30 days, including calls and data.
- **Locations:** Find stores in major towns like Ponta Delgada (São Miguel) and Angra do Heroísmo (Terceira).
- **Contact:** +351 16200

Vodafone

- **Overview:** Known for reliable service and competitive data plans.
- **Tourist SIM Cards:** Similar offerings to MEO, available at Vodafone

stores and some supermarkets.

- **Locations:** Vodafone store at Parque Atlântico Shopping Center, São Miguel.
- **Contact:** +351 16912

NOS

- **Overview:** Provides good coverage with an emphasis on data-heavy plans, ideal for visitors using smartphones for navigation and social media.
- **Tourist Plans:** Start at €20 for unlimited national calls and a substantial data allowance.
- **Locations:** NOS stores are located in larger centers like Ponta Delgada and Horta.
- **Contact:** +351 16990

Internet Access

While mobile data is an option, many visitors prefer WiFi for higher data usage activities. WiFi is widely available in hotels, cafes, and public spaces.

- **Public WiFi:** Major towns and tourist areas often have public WiFi, especially near tourist offices and main plazas.
- **Hotels and Accommodations:** Most offer free WiFi, though it's wise to check bandwidth if you plan on streaming or downloading large files.
- **Cafés and Restaurants:** Many provide free WiFi with a purchase. Look for signs or ask staff for login details.

Local Media

Staying informed about local news and events can enhance your travel experience in the Azores.

- **Newspapers:** 'Açoriano Oriental' and 'Diário dos Açores' are two major local newspapers that offer insight into local issues and events.
- **Television:** RTP-Açores provides regional programming with news and entertainment that reflects local culture.
- **Radio:** Antena 1 Açores offers a mix of news, talk, and music that is deeply embedded in the local context.

Tips for Communication

- **Language:** While Portuguese is the official language, English is widely spoken in tourist areas. Learning a few basic Portuguese phrases can be helpful in remote areas.
- **Charging Devices:** The Azores use European standard plugs (Type F, two-pin). Voltage is typically 220-240V. Bring an adapter if your devices use different standards.
- **Emergency Numbers:** Dial 112 for emergency services, accessible from any phone without a SIM card.

Money Matters: Currency, Banking, and Budgeting

Currency and Exchange

- **Currency Used:** The Euro (€) is the official currency in the Azores, as it is in mainland Portugal.
- **Exchanging Money:** It's best to exchange some currency before arriving,

but additional exchanges can be made at banks, airports, and hotels. However, airport and hotel rates are typically less favorable.

- **Locations for Exchange:**
- **Banco de Portugal** at Av. Infante Dom Henrique, Ponta Delgada, offers reliable exchange services.
- **Currency Exchange Offices:** Found at major airports such as João Paulo II Airport, Ponta Delgada.
- **Contact for Banco de Portugal:** +351 296 205 660

Banking and ATMs

- **Banking Hours:** Generally, banks in the Azores open from 8:30 AM to 3:00 PM, Monday through Friday.
- **ATM Accessibility:** ATMs, locally known as 'Multibancos', are widely available across all islands and are the most convenient way to withdraw cash.
- **Fees and Limits:** Typically, ATMs allow a withdrawal limit of €200-€400 per transaction. Fees vary by bank but expect to pay a small transaction fee if your home bank is outside of the Eurozone.
- **Important Locations for ATMs:**
- Major towns and tourist areas will have multiple ATMs. Look for ATMs attached to bank branches for the best reliability.
- **Central Ponta Delgada:** ATMs are readily available around Praça Gonçalo Velho Cabral.

Budgeting Tips
Daily Budget:
- **Low Budget:** €50-€70 per day can cover hostel accommodations, public transport, and meals from local markets or inexpensive cafes.

- **Moderate Budget:** €100-€150 per day allows for mid-range hotels, restaurant meals, some taxi rides, and entry fees for attractions.
- **High Budget:** Over €200 per day affords luxury accommodations, fine dining, car rentals, and guided tours.

Cost-Saving Tips:

- **Dining:** Eat where locals do; local bakeries, markets, and small-town diners offer authentic and less expensive meal options than tourist-heavy areas.
- **Accommodations:** Consider vacation rentals or rural tourism ('turismo rural') for longer stays, which can be more cost-effective and immersive.
- **Transport:** Using public transportation like buses can significantly save on costs compared to renting a car or frequent taxis.

Etiquette and Customs: Local Dos and Don'ts

Greetings and Social Interactions

- **Formalities:** Azoreans tend to be formal in their social interactions. When meeting someone, it is customary to shake hands. Among closer acquaintances, women may greet each other with two kisses on the cheeks, starting with the right cheek.
- **Addressing Others:** Use titles and surnames until invited to use first names. The titles "Senhor" (Mr.) and "Senhora" (Mrs.) are commonly used.
- **Small Talk:** When engaging in conversation, avoid controversial topics like politics. Instead, talking about the local scenery, food, and traditions is appreciated.

Dining Etiquette

- **Invitations:** If invited to a local's home, bring a small gift such as flowers or a bottle of wine. Arriving on time is important; punctuality reflects respect.
- **Table Manners:** Wait for the host to start eating before you begin. Passing food is done clockwise. Always say "thank you" at the end of the meal to show appreciation.
- **Eating Out:** Tipping is customary but not mandatory. Rounding up the bill or leaving an extra 5-10% is sufficient.

Dress Code

- **General Attire:** Dress codes are generally casual but neat. For churches or formal occasions, dress conservatively.
- **Footwear:** Comfortable walking shoes are essential due to the cobblestone streets and uneven pathways commonly found across the islands.
- **Beachwear:** Reserve swimsuits for beaches and pools. When visiting towns or dining out, it's respectful to cover up.

Public Behavior

- **Respect for Nature:** The Azores are known for their pristine environments. Always follow guidelines when hiking or visiting protected areas. Littering is frowned upon, as is disturbing wildlife.
- **Photography:** Always ask for permission before photographing local people, especially in smaller communities. In religious or sacred sites, observe and respect any photography restrictions.
- **Noise Levels:** Keep your voice down and avoid loud conversations, especially in small, quiet towns or on public transport.

Religious Observances

- **Church Attendance:** If attending a service, arrive on time and dress modestly. It's respectful to remain quiet and follow any local customs, such as standing or kneeling.
- **Festivals and Holy Days:** Participate respectfully in local festivals, which often have religious significance. Engaging with locals can enhance your experience, but always follow their lead on appropriate behavior.

Shopping and Bargaining

- **Market Etiquette:** While bargaining in markets is not common practice in the Azores, being polite and friendly can sometimes lead to a small discount. However, respect price tags, especially in formal shops and establishments.
- **Supporting Local Artisans:** Purchasing local crafts and products not only provides you with a unique souvenir but also supports the local economy. Always show appreciation for the craftsmanship.

Day Trips and Excursions

Planner for Day Trips: Must-Visit Nearby Attractions

São Miguel: Furnas Valley

- **Overview:** Furnas Valley is renowned for its geothermal activity, lush gardens, and unique culinary traditions.

Main Attractions:

- **Terra Nostra Garden:** Explore this botanical garden with its famous thermal pool.
- **Fumaroles and Hot Springs:** Witness the geothermal wonders and taste the locally cooked "Cozido das Furnas."
- **Location:** Furnas, São Miguel.
- **Cost:** Entry to Terra Nostra Garden is around €8 per person; Cozido meals average €25.
- **Travel Time:** About 45 minutes drive from Ponta Delgada.
- **Getting There:** Accessible by car or public bus. Parking available near major attractions.
- **Contact:** Terra Nostra Garden - +351 296 549 090

Terceira: Algar do Carvão and Angra do Heroísmo

- **Overview:** A day exploring volcanic caves followed by a visit to a UNESCO World Heritage city.

Main Attractions:

- **Algar do Carvão:** An ancient lava tube that you can enter and explore.
- **Angra do Heroísmo:** Historic city center with museums, churches, and seaside promenades.
- **Location:** Central Terceira.
- **Cost:** Algar do Carvão entry is about €6; museums and other attractions in Angra may have separate fees.
- **Travel Time:** Algar do Carvão is 20 minutes from Angra do Heroísmo.
- **Getting There:** Best reached by rental car; public buses are available but less frequent.
- **Contact:** Algar do Carvão - +351 295 212 992

Pico: Mountain Climb and Wine Tasting

- **Overview:** Conquer Portugal's highest peak and unwind with local wines.

Main Attractions:

- **Mount Pico:** Guided climbs to the summit for breathtaking views.
- **Pico Wine Country:** Visit local vineyards for tours and tastings.
- **Location:** Pico Island.
- **Cost:** Mountain guides around €30-€50; wine tastings vary, typically

around €10.

- **Travel Time:** Varies across the island; the mountain is about 30 minutes from Madalena.
- **Getting There:** Mount Pico is best accessed by car; vineyards offer tours often with transportation.
- **Contact:** Pico Mountain House - +351 292 642 634

Faial: Capelinhos Volcano and Coastal Trails

- **Overview:** Visit the site of the last major volcanic eruption in the Azores and explore stunning coastal scenery.

Main Attractions:

- **Capelinhos Volcano:** Learn about the 1957 eruption at the visitor center and walk the ash-covered landscapes.
- **Coastal Trails:** Hike along the dramatic cliffs and views of the Atlantic.
- **Location:** Western Faial.
- **Cost:** Capelinhos visitor center is about €4; trails are free.
- **Travel Time:** Around 30 minutes drive from Horta.
- **Getting There:** Accessible by car; limited public transport options to the volcano.
- **Contact:** Capelinhos Visitor Center - +351 292 200 470

São Jorge: Fajãs Exploration

- **Overview:** Discover the unique fajãs, flat coastal areas formed by ancient lava flows, which host a variety of microclimates.

Main Attractions:

- **Fajã dos Cubres:** Stunning lagoon and popular spot for bird watching.
- **Fajã de Santo Cristo:** Famous for its clams and tranquil setting.
- **Location:** Northern coast of São Jorge.
- **Cost:** Free access to fajãs; local dining experiences vary.
- **Travel Time:** About 1 hour from Velas.
- **Getting There:** Best reached by car; hiking options available for the adventurous.
- **Contact:** Local tourism office in Velas - +351 295 430 000

Longer Journeys: Exploring Beyond the Immediate

Multi-Island Hopping Adventure

- **Overview:** A tour across several islands, each with its distinct character, landscape, and traditions.

Itinerary:

- **Day 1-3: São Miguel** – Start with the island's geothermal wonders and lush landscapes.
- **Day 4-5: Terceira** – Explore the historical sites and volcanic caves.
- **Day 6-7: Pico** – Ascend Portugal's highest peak and visit the famous wine vineyards.
- **Day 8-9: Faial** – Discover the Capelinhos Volcano and the charming town of Horta.
- **Day 10: São Jorge** – Hike the stunning fajãs and sample local clams.
- **Cost:** Varies by chosen accommodations and activities; budget at least €1500-€2000 for a comprehensive 10-day trip including inter-island flights and accommodations.

- **Travel Tips:** Book flights and ferries between islands in advance, especially during the high season. Consider guided tours for specific activities like mountain climbing or scuba diving.
- **Contact Information:** Azores Airlines for inter-island flights - +351 296 209 720; Local tour operators for guided excursions.

Eastern Group Cultural and Natural Heritage Tour

- **Overview:** An in-depth exploration of the eastern group of the Azores, focusing on São Miguel and Santa Maria, showcasing a blend of cultural heritage and natural beauty.

Itinerary:

- **São Miguel:** Spend several days visiting places like Furnas, Nordeste, and the Ribeira dos Caldeirões for an in-depth look at local traditions and natural sights.
- **Santa Maria:** Known for its white sandy beaches and vineyards, spend 3-4 days here engaging in activities like snorkeling, historical tours, and wine tasting.
- **Cost:** Approximately €100-€150 per day, including accommodations, meals, and transport.
- **Getting There:** Regular flights from São Miguel to Santa Maria with SATA Air Açores.
- **Special Notes:** Santa Maria offers a slower pace of life and fewer tourists, ideal for those looking to unwind and experience genuine Azorean culture.
- **Contact:** Tourism offices on both islands for detailed maps and event schedules.

Western Islands Nature Escape

- **Overview:** This journey focuses on the islands of Flores and Corvo, offering some of the most dramatic landscapes and excellent opportunities for bird watching and nature hikes.

Itinerary:

- **Flores:** Visit the numerous waterfalls, lakes, and cliffs. Key spots include Rocha dos Bordões and the seven crater lakes.
- **Corvo:** Spend a day or two in this tiny island community, with a guided tour of Caldeirão crater and birdwatching excursions.
- **Cost:** Expect to spend about €100 per day, including local guesthouse stays, food, and guided tours.
- **Travel Tips:** Travel to Flores by plane from São Miguel or Faial, then take a ferry or a local flight to Corvo. Accommodations are limited, so book well in advance.
- **Contact:** Flores and Corvo local tourism offices for booking tours and accommodations.

Hidden Gems: Off the Beaten Track

São Miguel: Lagoa do Congro

- **Overview:** Cuddled amidst lush greenery, Lagoa do Congro is a secluded lake formed in a volcanic crater, known for its stunning emerald green waters.
- **Location:** Access via a dirt road and a short hike from the main road near Vila Franca do Campo.

- **Cost:** Free entry.
- **Getting There:** Best accessed by car; parking available near the trailhead. The hike down to the lake takes about 15 minutes.
- **What to Do:** Ideal for hiking and nature photography. The serene setting is perfect for picnicking and bird-watching.
- **Contact:** São Miguel tourism office - +351 296 308 400 for updates on trail conditions.

Terceira: Algar do Carvão

- **Overview:** An ancient lava tube that visitors can enter, featuring a subterranean garden and a lake deep inside the earth.
- **Location:** In the heart of Terceira, near Angra do Heroísmo.
- **Cost:** Approximately €8 for adults.
- **Getting There:** Access is via the road towards Praia da Vitória, with clear signage from the highway.
- **Hours:** Open seasonally, typically from April to October, with guided tours available.
- **Contact:** +351 295 212 992 for tour schedules and special event information.

Pico: Cachorro

- **Overview:** Cachorro in Pico is famed for its wine and unique volcanic rock formations that create natural swimming pools.
- **Location:** North coast of Pico, near the village of Madalena.
- **Cost:** Free access to the pools and coastal areas.
- **Getting There:** Roughly 15 minutes drive from Madalena. Street parking available.
- **What to Do:** Swimming, snorkeling in the natural pools, and exploring the rocky coast.

- **Contact:** Pico tourism office - +351 292 642 444 for more details on local guidelines and safety.

Flores: Poço do Bacalhau

- **Overview:** A breathtaking 90-meter waterfall that cascades into a clear, natural pool, surrounded by lush vegetation.
- **Location:** Near Fajã Grande on the western coast of Flores.
- **Cost:** Free entry.
- **Getting There:** Accessible by car with a parking area near the trailhead; a short walk leads directly to the waterfall.
- **What to Do:** Swimming and photography are popular, as well as hiking along the nearby trails.
- **Contact:** Flores tourism office - +351 292 542 372 to inquire about weather conditions and the best times to visit.

São Jorge: Fajã de Santo Cristo

- **Overview:** This fajã is renowned for its stunning scenery, isolation, and the unique ecosystem, including a lagoon famous for clam harvesting.
- **Location:** Accessible via a footpath from Topo or by a rough, unpaved road suitable for 4x4 vehicles.
- **Cost:** Free entry.
- **Getting There:** The hike from Topo takes approximately 2 hours one way, offering spectacular coastal views.
- **What to Do:** Ideal for hiking, bird-watching, and enjoying local seafood, especially the clams.
- **Contact:** São Jorge tourism office - +351 295 430 000 for guide services and environmental regulations.

Special Interests

Eco-Tourism: Sustainable Travel Options

Sustainable Accommodations

- **Overview:** Choose from a variety of eco-lodges, green hotels, and locally owned guesthouses that use renewable energy, recycle waste, and offer organic local food.

Recommended Places:

- **Casa do Valle (São Miguel):** Solar-powered heating and organic breakfasts. Located at Rua do Valle 17, Furnas. Contact: +351 296 584.
- **Hotel do Canal (Faial):** Eco-certified hotel that emphasizes recycling and energy efficiency. Located at Largo Dr. Manuel de Arriaga, Horta. Contact: +351 292 202 120.
- **Cost:** Prices vary; eco-lodges typically range from €80 to €200 per night depending on the season and amenities.

Eco-Friendly Activities

- **Nature Tours:** Participate in guided tours that focus on education and conservation, minimizing impact on the environment.

- **Ilha Verde Walking Tours (São Miguel):** Offers guided walks through protected areas with local environmentalists. Contact: +351 296 628.
- **OceanEmotion (Terceira):** Whale watching and wildlife tours led by marine biologists. Located in Angra do Heroísmo. Contact: +351 295 098.
- **Cost:** Approximately €45 for half-day tours to €90 for full-day experiences.

Supporting Local Conservation Efforts

- **Volunteering:** Engage in volunteer programs that contribute to habitat restoration, wildlife monitoring, or community farming.
- **Montanha do Pico Nature Reserve:** Offers opportunities to help with reforestation and endemic species protection. Contact: +351 292 207 375 for volunteer opportunities.
- **Adopt Sustainable Practices:** Follow 'leave no trace' principles during hikes, use reusable water bottles, and choose digital over printed materials.

Transportation

- **Public Transport and Electric Rentals:** Utilize eco-friendly transport options available on the islands.
- **São Miguel Electric Bus Service:** Operates across major routes in Ponta Delgada and surrounding areas.
- **Eco Rent (Pico):** Provides electric cars and bikes for rent. Located in Madalena. Contact: +351 292 623.
- **Cost:** Bus fares around €1-€3; electric car rentals from €40 per day.

Local Products and Crafts

- **Supporting Local Artisans:** Purchase locally-made products and crafts which help reduce carbon footprint and support the local economy.

- **Mercado da Graça (São Miguel):** A marketplace where local artisans sell handmade goods. Located in Ponta Delgada.
- **Products Include:** Hand-woven baskets, ceramic crafts, and homemade jams.
- **Cost:** Prices depend on the product, ranging from €5 for small items to over €100 for elaborate handicrafts.

Eco-Tourism Policies and Practices

- **Government and Community Initiatives:** Stay informed about the local policies that promote sustainability.
- **Azores Certification for Sustainable Tourism:** Many businesses adhere to strict guidelines to maintain this certification, ensuring they meet environmental standards.
- **Contribution:** Consider contributing to local environmental funds or initiatives that work towards conservation and sustainability.

Wellness and Health: Spas and Retreats

Thermal Spas and Wellness Centers

Furnas Spa (São Miguel)

- **Overview:** Located in the geothermal area of Furnas, this spa utilizes the region's natural hot springs to offer a range of therapeutic treatments.
- **Treatments Offered:** Mineral baths, mud treatments, and hydrotherapy.
- **Address:** Rua das Caldeiras, Furnas, São Miguel.
- **Cost:** Entry starts at €20 for access to pools; treatments range from €50 to €100.
- **Getting There:** Approximately 45 minutes drive from Ponta Delgada.

Free parking available on site.
- **Contact:** +351 296 584 256
- **Note:** Booking in advance is recommended, especially during the tourist season.

Terra Nostra Garden Hotel (São Miguel)

- **Overview:** Part of the Terra Nostra Garden, this hotel features a thermal swimming pool and wellness treatments amidst a botanical garden.
- **Treatments Offered:** Aromatherapy, massages, and facial treatments.
- **Address:** Rua Padre José Jacinto Botelho, Furnas, São Miguel.
- **Cost:** Hotel guests get free access to the pool; non-guests pay €8. Spa treatments start at €45.
- **Getting There:** Situated in Furnas, well-signposted from main roads.
- **Contact:** +351 296 549 090
- **Note:** The thermal pool is a highlight, rich in iron and other minerals.

Holistic Retreats

Pico Holistic Retreat Center (Pico)

- **Overview:** Focused on holistic wellness, this retreat offers programs that include yoga, meditation, and nature walks.
- **Programs Offered:** Yoga retreats, meditation sessions, and nutritional workshops.
- **Address:** Caminho de Baixo, São Roque, Pico.
- **Cost:** Prices for retreats start at €750 per week, including accommodation, meals, and activities.
- **Getting There:** About 30 minutes drive from Pico Airport. Transport can be arranged by the retreat center.

- **Contact:** +351 292 642 443
- **Note:** Ideal for those looking for a comprehensive wellness experience in a tranquil setting.

Graciosa Wellness Resort (Graciosa)

- **Overview:** Offers a blend of wellness treatments and relaxation opportunities in a quiet, unspoiled environment.
- **Treatments Offered:** Sea water therapies, beauty treatments, and stress relief programs.
- **Address:** Rua da Barra, Santa Cruz da Graciosa.
- **Cost:** Day passes to the wellness area start at €30. Room rates with wellness packages start at €120 per night.
- **Getting There:** Accessible by ferry from São Miguel or Terceira, followed by a short drive from the port.
- **Contact:** +351 295 730 500
- **Note:** Their sea therapy sessions are highly recommended for their rejuvenating properties.

Fitness and Detox Programs

Faial Fitness Retreat (Faial)

- **Overview:** Combines fitness activities with relaxation techniques against the backdrop of Faial's dramatic landscapes.
- **Programs Offered:** Guided hikes, water aerobics, and detox diets.
- **Address:** Estrada Transversal, Horta, Faial.
- **Cost:** A 5-day fitness retreat package starts at €500, inclusive of meals and accommodation.
- **Getting There:** Approximately 20 minutes from Horta Airport by car.
- **Contact:** +351 292 292 308

- **Note:** Customizable programs are available depending on fitness levels and health goals.

Historical Sites: A Deep Dive into the Past

The Azores archipelago, rich with history and culture, offers a treasure trove of historical sites that tell the tales of its past—from its discovery in the 15th century to its strategic role in World War II and beyond.

Angra do Heroísmo (Terceira Island)

Overview: A UNESCO World Heritage site, Angra played a crucial role as a linking point between Europe, Africa, and the Americas during the Age of Discovery.
   Main Attractions:

- **Sé Cathedral:** Built in 1570, this cathedral is a blend of Gothic and Baroque architectural styles.

Fortaleza de São João Baptista: An imposing fortress constructed in the 16th century to protect against pirate attacks.

- **Address:** Central Angra do Heroísmo, Terceira.
- **Cost:** Cathedral is free to enter; Fortaleza tour costs €5.
- **Getting There:** Angra is accessible by bus or car from any part of Terceira. Public parking available near major sites.
- **Contact:** Angra tourism office - +351 295 401 700 for guided tour schedules.

Lajes do Pico (Pico Island)

Overview: This village was a whaling center in the 19th and 20th centuries, with its whaling industry playing a vital part in the island's economy.

Main Attractions:

- **Whalers' Museum (Museu dos Baleeiros):** Displays related to the history of whaling, including boats, tools, and photographs.
- **Address:** Rua dos Baleeiros, Lajes do Pico, Pico Island.
- **Cost:** €2.50 per person.
- **Getting There:** Lajes do Pico is about 30 minutes drive from Madalena. Free parking available near the museum.
- **Contact:** +351 292 672 276 for museum hours and special exhibits.

Ponta Delgada (São Miguel Island)

Overview: The capital of São Miguel, known for its historic buildings and monuments dating back to the 17th century.

Main Attractions:

- **Portas da Cidade:** The iconic triple-arched gateway that has stood since 1783.
- **Carlos Machado Museum:** Housed in a former convent, this museum showcases Azorean art, history, and natural history.
- **Address:** Central Ponta Delgada, São Miguel.
- **Cost:** Free entry to Portas da Cidade; Museum entry is €4.
- **Getting There:** Central location in Ponta Delgada, easily walkable from

most parts of the city.

- **Contact:** Ponta Delgada tourism office - +351 296 308 400 for museum details.

Ribeira Grande (São Miguel Island)

Overview: Known for its 16th-century architecture and the historic influence of Jewish settlers in the Azores.

Main Attractions:

- **Bridge of Eight Arches (Ponte dos Oito Arcos):** Historic bridge that is a significant landmark of the town.
- **Arquipélago Contemporary Arts Centre:** Offers exhibitions in a renovated 19th-century alcohol factory.
- **Address:** Ribeira Grande, São Miguel.
- **Cost:** Free to explore the town; Arts Centre has varying ticket prices.
- **Getting There:** About 15 minutes drive north from Ponta Delgada.
- **Contact:** Ribeira Grande tourism office - +351 296 470 730 for current exhibitions.

São Jorge (São Jorge Island)

Overview: This island is dotted with fortifications that defended against pirate attacks in the early modern period.

Main Attractions:

- **Fort of Santa Cruz:** Located in the village of Velas, this fort offers panoramic views of the harbor.

- **Address:** Velas, São Jorge.
- **Cost:** Free entry.
- **Getting There:** Velas can be reached by car or public transport from other parts of São Jorge.
- **Contact:** São Jorge tourism office - +351 295 430 000 for more historical insight.

Essential Information

Contact Information: Emergency, Consular, and Local Services

Emergency Services

- **Emergency Number:** 112 (for police, fire, and medical emergencies)
- **Details:** This number can be dialed from any phone, free of charge. Operators are trained to respond to calls in multiple languages, including English.

Health Services

Hospital do Divino Espírito Santo (Ponta Delgada, São Miguel)

- **Address:** Rua de São Gonçalo, 9500-343 Ponta Delgada, São Miguel.
- **Contact:** +351 296 203 000
- **Services:** Emergency care, specialist consultations, and inpatient services.

Hospital de Santo Espírito (Angra do Heroísmo, Terceira)

- **Address:** Canada Nova, 9700-045 Angra do Heroísmo, Terceira.
- **Contact:** +351 295 403 200
- **Services:** Full range of medical services including emergency and

elective treatments.

Police Stations

PSP Ponta Delgada (Public Security Police)

- **Address:** Avenida Roberto Ivens, Ponta Delgada, São Miguel.
- **Contact:** +351 296 282 022
- **Details:** Offers tourist support services and immediate response to public disturbances or reports.

GNR Angra do Heroísmo (National Republican Guard)

- **Address:** Rua da Sé, Angra do Heroísmo, Terceira.
- **Contact:** +351 295 206 860
- **Details:** Provides law enforcement, traffic regulation, and public safety services.

Consular Services

U.S. Consulate in Ponta Delgada

- **Address:** Avenida Príncipe do Mónaco, 9500-237 Ponta Delgada, São Miguel.
- **Contact:** +351 296 308 000
- **Services:** Assistance to U.S. citizens including passport services, consular reports of birth abroad, and emergency assistance.

British Honorary Consulate in Ponta Delgada

- **Address:** Rua São João 33, 9500-107 Ponta Delgada, São Miguel.
- **Contact:** +351 296 286 887
- **Services:** Limited consular services including emergency assistance to British nationals.

Local Tourist Offices

São Miguel Tourist Office

- **Address:** Avenida Infante Dom Henrique, 9504-769 Ponta Delgada, São Miguel.
- **Contact:** +351 296 205 760
- **Services:** Information on local attractions, accommodation, events, and transport.
- **Terceira Tourist Office**
- **Address:** Rua da Sé, 9700-191 Angra do Heroísmo, Terceira.
- **Contact:** +351 295 216 480
- **Services:** Provides maps, brochures, event information, and guidance on local tours.

Additional Useful Contacts
Roadside Assistance (Automóvel Club de Portugal)

- **Contact:** +351 707 201 280
- **Services:** Roadside assistance, towing services, and help with vehicle-related issues.
- **Maritime Tourist Assistance**
- **Contact:** +351 214 401 919
- **Services:** Assistance for maritime accidents and emergencies.

Language Help

Basic Greetings and Courtesies

- **Olá (oh-lah)**: Hello
- **Bom dia (bong dee-ah)**: Good morning
- **Boa tarde (boh-ah tar-deh)**: Good afternoon
- **Boa noite (boh-ah noy-teh)**: Good evening/night
- **Adeus (ah-deh-oosh)**: Goodbye
- **Por favor (por fah-vor)**: Please
- **Obrigado (ob-ree-gah-doh) / Obrigada (ob-ree-gah-dah)**: Thank you (male/female)
- **Desculpe (desh-kul-peh)**: Excuse me/Sorry
- **Sim (seem)**: Yes
- **Não (now)**: No

Directions and Travel

- **Onde fica...? (on-deh fee-kah)**: Where is...?
- **Esquerda (esh-kehr-dah)**: Left
- **Direita (dee-ray-tah)**: Right
- **Em frente (eng fren-teh)**: Straight ahead
- **Para trás (par-ah trash)**: Backwards
- **Estação (eh-stah-sow)**: Station
- **Aeroporto (ah-eh-ro-por-toh)**: Airport
- **Paragem de autocarro (par-ah-geng deh ow-to-car-roh)**: Bus stop
- **Táxi (tah-shee)**: Taxi
- **Aluguer de carros (a-loo-gher deh car-rosh)**: Car rental

Dining and Food

- **Restaurante (reh-stow-ran-teh)**: Restaurant
- **Menu (meh-noo)**: Menu

- **Conta (kon-tah)**: Bill
- **Garfo (gar-foh)**: Fork
- **Colher (kol-yer)**: Spoon
- **Faca (fah-kah)**: Knife
- **Prato (prah-toh)**: Plate/Dish
- **Sal (sal)**: Salt
- **Pimenta (pee-men-tah)**: Pepper
- **Água (ah-gwah)**: Water

Shopping

- **Quanto custa? (kwan-toh koos-tah)**: How much does it cost?
- **Loja (loh-jah)**: Shop
- **Preço (preh-soh)**: Price
- **Desconto (dehs-kon-toh)**: Discount
- **Tamanho (tah-mahn-yoh)**: Size
- **Provar (proh-var)**: To try on
- **Aberto (ah-ber-toh)**: Open
- **Fechado (feh-shah-doh)**: Closed

Emergency and Health

- **Ajuda (ah-joo-dah)**: Help
- **Polícia (po-lee-see-ah)**: Police
- **Médico (meh-dee-koh)**: Doctor
- **Farmácia (far-mah-see-ah)**: Pharmacy
- **Hospital (hos-pee-tal)**: Hospital
- **Estou doente (eh-stow doy-en-teh)**: I am sick
- **Acidente (ah-see-den-teh)**: Accident
- **Farmácia de serviço (far-mah-see-ah deh ser-vee-soh)**: On-call pharmacy

Social Interactions

- **Como se chama? (ko-mo seh shah-mah)**: What is your name?
- **Prazer em conhecê-lo/a (prah-zer eng ko-nuh-seh-loh/ah)**: Pleased to meet you (male/female)
- **De onde é? (deh on-deh eh)**: Where are you from?
- **Fala inglês? (fah-lah een-glesh)**: Do you speak English?
- **Pode ajudar-me? (po-deh ah-joo-dar-meh)**: Can you help me?

Itineraries

3-Day Itinerary for the Azores: A Whirlwind Tour

Day 1: Ponta Delgada and Western São Miguel

Morning:

- **Arrival in Ponta Delgada**
- Start your Azorean adventure by exploring the charming streets of Ponta Delgada. Visit the **Portas da Cidade (City Gates)** and the **Church of São Sebastião** for a taste of local architecture and history.
- **Breakfast** at **La Bamba Bistro** - Enjoy Azorean delicacies with a modern twist.

Afternoon:

- **Sete Cidades Tour**
- Drive or join a guided tour to the stunning **Sete Cidades**, a massive volcanic crater with twin lakes that are a legend in the Azores. The viewpoint from **Vista do Rei** offers breathtaking views.
- **Lunch** at **O Poejo** restaurant in Sete Cidades, famous for local stews and fresh fish.

Evening:

- **Return to Ponta Delgada**
- Enjoy a leisurely dinner at **A Tasca** where traditional Azorean dishes meet contemporary preparation.
- **Accommodation:** Stay at **Hotel Marina Atlântico** on the seaside avenue in Ponta Delgada for central access and beautiful ocean views.

Day 2: Furnas and Nordeste

Morning:

- **Depart for Furnas**
- After breakfast, make the scenic drive to Furnas, known for its hot springs and botanical gardens.
- Visit the **Terra Nostra Botanical Garden**, take a thermal bath in its iron-rich waters, and walk among hundreds of endemic plants.

Afternoon:

- **Lunch** at **Terra Nostra Garden Hotel** enjoying "Cozido das Furnas" – a local dish cooked by volcanic steam.
- Post-lunch, head to the eastern side of São Miguel to explore the lush landscapes and rugged coastlines of **Nordeste**. Stop at the picturesque viewpoints like **Miradouro da Ponta do Sossego** and **Miradouro da Ponta da Madrugada**.

Evening:

- **Dinner** at **Restaurante São Pedro**, which offers seafood right by the ocean.
- **Accommodation:** Spend the night at **Furnas Boutique Hotel** in Furnas to experience more of the town's thermal springs.

Day 3: Vila Franca do Campo and Departure

Morning:

- **Ilhéu de Vila Franca do Campo**
- Take a morning boat trip to the islet of Vila Franca do Campo, a nature reserve with a stunning circular lagoon perfect for snorkeling and swimming.
- **Breakfast** or early lunch at **Café Céu Azul** in Vila Franca, known for its pastries and local coffee.

Afternoon:

- **Explore more of Vila Franca do Campo**, including the historical **Church of São Miguel Arcanjo** and the local market.
- **Late Lunch** at **O Silva** where the ocean meets your plate with dishes like grilled limpets and octopus salad.

Evening:

- **Departure from Ponta Delgada**
- Depending on your flight time, grab a quick dinner at **Mercado da Graça** in Ponta Delgada, where you can sample a variety of local foods in a lively market setting.

Accommodation Tip:

For those who prefer a tranquil rural setting, consider staying at a local farmhouse or "quinta", which are often available around Vila Franca do Campo.

7-Day Itinerary: São Miguel to Pico - A Journey Through the Azores

Day 1: Arrival and Exploration in Ponta Delgada, São Miguel

Morning:

- **Arrival at João Paulo II Airport**, Ponta Delgada.
- **Check-in** at **Hotel Casa Hintze Ribeiro**, known for its central location and charming decor.

Afternoon:

- **Lunch** at **Restaurante Nacional** for a taste of traditional Azorean dishes.
- **Explore Downtown Ponta Delgada:** Visit the **Portas da Cidade, Fortress of São Brás**, and stroll along the marina.

Evening:

- **Dinner** at **A Tasca**, famous for its seafood tapas.
- **Relax** with a casual walk on the seaside promenade.

Day 2: Sete Cidades and Thermal Pools

Morning:

- **Drive to Sete Cidades**, stopping at various viewpoints like **Vista do Rei** for spectacular views of the twin lakes.
- **Kayaking** on the blue and green lakes.

Afternoon:

- **Lunch** at **Lagoa Azul Restaurant** overlooking the lake.
- **Visit Caldeira Velha**, experiencing the warm waterfall and natural swimming pools.

Evening:

- Return to Ponta Delgada.
- **Dinner** at **O Giro** - Praised for its steaks and local wines.

Day 3: Northeast São Miguel

Morning:

- **Head to Nordeste**, visiting the lush landscapes and the unique waterfalls at **Ribeira dos Caldeirões Natural Park**.
- **Breakfast** at a local bakery in Nordeste.

Afternoon:

- **Picnic lunch** in the park.
- **Explore the lighthouses** and cliffside viewpoints.

Evening:

- Drive back to Ponta Delgada.
- **Dinner** and overnight at **Hotel Casa Hintze Ribeiro**.

Day 4: Travel to Pico Island

Morning:

- **Flight to Pico Island**.
- **Check-in** at **Aldeia da Fonte Hotel**, a nature-integrated hotel by the sea.

Afternoon:

- **Lunch** at the hotel's restaurant.
- **Visit to Lava Caves (Gruta das Torres)**, exploring Pico's volcanic underground.

Evening:

- **Dinner** at **Cella Bar**, enjoying local wines and gourmet snacks.

Day 5: Mountain Hike and Vineyards

Morning:

- **Climb Mount Pico**, guided hike to the summit of Portugal's highest mountain (pre-book guide).
- **Picnic breakfast** on the mountain.

Afternoon:

- Descend and **lunch** at **A Tasquinha** in Madalena.

- **Tour the Pico Vineyard Culture**, a UNESCO World Heritage site, tasting Azorean wine.

Evening:

- **Relax** at the hotel or explore Madalena's coastal area.
- **Dinner** at the hotel.

Day 6: Whale Watching and São Roque

Morning:

- **Whale watching tour** from Madalena (pre-book this popular activity).
- **Breakfast** on board.

Afternoon:

- **Lunch** at **Ancoradouro Restaurant** in São Roque.
- **Visit the São Roque Museum** and spend time at the natural swimming pools.

Evening:

- **Casual dinner** at a local pizzeria.
- **Stargazing** session back at the hotel or at a nearby observatory.

Day 7: Leisure Day and Departure

Morning:

- **Leisurely breakfast** at the hotel.
- **Relax** on a volcanic beach or revisit a favorite spot.

Afternoon:

- **Lunch** in Madalena.
- **Last-minute shopping** for local crafts and wines.

Evening:

- **Departure from Pico Airport**, or extend the stay exploring nearby islands like Faial or São Jorge.

14-Day Expansive Itinerary in the Azores: Deep Exploration of Each Island

Day 1-2: Arrival and Ponta Delgada, São Miguel

Day 1:

- **Arrival** at João Paulo II Airport, Ponta Delgada.
- **Check-in:** Hotel Azor.
- **Explore** the city, focusing on historic sites like **Portas da Cidade** and **Fortress of São Brás**.

Day 2:

- **Full-day tour** of the west side, including **Sete Cidades**, and **Ferraria** where the ocean heats naturally.

Day 3-4: Furnas and Northeast São Miguel

Day 3:

- **Visit** Furnas to explore hot springs and the **Terra Nostra Botanical Garden**.
- **Lunch** with Cozido das Furnas, cooked underground by volcanic steam.

Day 4:

- **Drive** to Nordeste, visiting the viewpoints and enjoying the lush landscapes.
- **Overnight** in Ponta Delgada.

Day 5: Travel to Terceira

Day 5:

- **Flight to Terceira.**
- **Check-in:** Pousada de Angra do Heroísmo.
- **Explore** Angra do Heroísmo, a UNESCO World Heritage site.

Day 6-7: Exploring Terceira

Day 6:

- **Visit** Monte Brasil and the Algar do Carvão volcanic pit.
- **Evening** at local tascas for dinner.

Day 7:

- **Leisure day** exploring local markets and beaches.
- **Nighttime** ghost tour of Angra.

Day 8: Pico Island

Day 8:

- **Morning flight** to Pico.
- **Check-in:** Aldeia da Fonte Hotel.
- **Afternoon visit** to the Whaler's Museum in Lajes.

Day 9-10: Pico's Natural Beauty and Vineyards

Day 9:

- **Climb Pico Mountain**, guided tour.
- **Relax** in the evening at the hotel.

Day 10:

- **Tour** the UNESCO protected vineyard landscape.
- **Wine tasting** session at local adegas.

Day 11: Faial Island

Day 11:

- **Morning ferry** to Faial.
- **Visit** the Capelinhos Volcano Interpretation Centre.
- **Explore** Horta and the famous Peter Café Sport.

Day 12: São Jorge

Day 12:

- **Ferry to São Jorge**.
- **Check-in** at a local guesthouse.
- **Explore** Fajãs and local cheese factories.

Day 13: Leisure Day in São Jorge

Day 13:

- **Hiking** in São Jorge's unique terrain or a **kayaking** trip along the coast.
- **Relax** and enjoy local cuisine.

Day 14: Return to São Miguel and Departure

Day 14:

- **Return flight** to São Miguel.
- **Last-minute shopping** in Ponta Delgada.
- **Departure.**

Cultural Enthusiasts' Itinerary

Day 1-2: São Miguel - The Cultural Heart

Day 1:

- **Arrival** in Ponta Delgada, São Miguel.
- **Check-in:** Hotel Senhora da Rosa, traditional elegance meets modern comfort.
- **Explore** historical downtown: Visit **Carlos Machado Museum**, known for its collections reflecting Azorean culture.

Day 2:

- **Morning visit** to the **São Brás Military Museum**.
- **Afternoon:** Explore local markets and **Arruda Pineapple Plantation** to learn about traditional agriculture.
- **Evening:** Attend a local music performance or a festival if available.

Day 3-4: Terceira - The Historical Stage

Day 3:

- **Flight to Terceira.**
- **Check-in:** Pousada de Angra do Heroísmo in the heart of the historic city.
- **Walking tour** of Angra do Heroísmo, a UNESCO World Heritage Site.

Day 4:

- **Visit** to the **Museum of Angra do Heroísmo** which houses significant historical artifacts.
- **Afternoon:** Join a workshop on traditional Azorean lace or pottery.
- **Evening:** Experience a traditional bullfight or street festival (seasonal).

Day 5-6: Pico - The Island of Craftsmen

Day 5:

- **Morning ferry** to Pico.
- **Visit** the **Whaler's Museum** in Lajes to understand the historical significance of whaling in Azorean culture.
- **Afternoon:** Explore the vineyards of Pico, a UNESCO site, including wine tasting and learning about local wine-making.

Day 6:

- **Workshop participation:** Spend a day with a local artisan crafting

Azorean instruments or boat models.

- **Evening:** Casual dinner at a local tavern enjoying Pico cheese and wine.

Day 7: Faial - The Blue Island

Day 7:

- **Morning ferry** to Faial.
- **Visit** the **Horta Regional Museum** with exhibits on the maritime history and cycles of economic boom and bust.
- **Afternoon:** Explore the marina painted with murals by visiting sailors.
- **Evening:** Attend a local storytelling session or a guitar night at Café Peter Sport.

Day 8-9: São Jorge - The Land of Fajãs

Day 8:

- **Ferry to São Jorge.**
- **Explore** the unique **Fajãs** with a local guide discussing their creation and cultural importance.
- **Visit** a local cooperative to see cheese-making.

Day 9:

- **Hiking** through traditional footpaths connecting different fajãs, exploring small chapels and watermills along the way.
- **Evening:** Participate in a community dinner, often accompanied by folklore music and dances.

Day 10-11: Back to São Miguel

Day 10:

- **Return to São Miguel.**
- **Visit** the town of **Ribeira Grande**, with its baroque architecture and **Museu Casa do Arcano** to see local art.
- **Evening:** Explore local dining with emphasis on Azorean cuisine.

Day 11:

- **Leisure day** in São Miguel with options to visit artisan studios or additional local museums.
- **Final night:** Attend a concert or festival showcasing Azorean music and dance.

Departure Day:

- **Departure from São Miguel,** enriched with the cultural heritage of the Azores.

Adventure Seekers' Itinerary

Day 1-2: São Miguel - The Adventure Hub

Day 1:

- **Arrival in Ponta Delgada**, São Miguel.
- **Check-in**: Azor Hotel, known for its modern amenities and proximity

to adventure sports facilities.

- **Afternoon**: Kayaking in the **Lagoa das Sete Cidades**, exploring both the Green and Blue lakes.
- **Evening**: Briefing on activities and dinner at **A Terra Azor** featuring fresh local ingredients.

Day 2:

- **Morning**: Canyoning in **Ribeira dos Caldeirões**, an exhilarating experience navigating waterfalls and streams.
- **Afternoon**: Mountain biking through the trails around **Furnas**, known for their stunning views and challenging terrain.
- **Evening**: Relax in the **Furnas hot springs**, a natural way to soothe muscles after a day of activity.

Day 3-4: Terceira - The Historical Adventure

Day 3:

- **Flight to Terceira.**
- **Check-in**: Angra Garden Hotel, ideally located in the historical center of Angra do Heroísmo.
- **Afternoon**: Dive in the waters off **Monte Brasil**, exploring underwater volcanic formations and marine life.
- **Evening**: Traditional dinner in Angra, enjoying local seafood dishes.

Day 4:

- **Morning**: Hike the **Mistérios Negros** trail, meandering through lush forests and past volcanic vents.
- **Afternoon**: Paragliding off the cliffs of Serra do Cume, offering

panoramic views of the patchwork landscape.

- **Evening**: Attend a local festival if available, experiencing Terceira's vibrant culture.

Day 5-6: Pico - The Peak of Adventure

Day 5:

- **Morning ferry** to Pico.
- **Check-in**: Lava Homes on Pico's north coast, known for their stunning architecture and views.
- **Afternoon**: Climb **Mount Pico**, Portugal's highest peak, for an unforgettable sunset experience.
- **Evening**: Overnight in a mountain hut, under the stars.

Day 6:

- **Morning**: Complete the descent from Mount Pico.
- **Afternoon**: Whale watching tour to see some of the ocean's most majestic creatures in their natural habitat.
- **Evening**: Wine tasting at a local vineyard, relaxing after the day's adventures.

Day 7: Faial - The Blue Island Adventure

Day 7:

- **Morning ferry** to Faial.
- **Morning**: Dive the submerged volcanic crater near **Cabo de São**

Sebastião, exploring sea caves and encountering diverse marine life.
- **Afternoon**: Explore the **Caldeira do Faial** on a guided hike, one of the most iconic landscapes in the Azores.
- **Evening**: Enjoy a casual dinner at Peter Café Sport, an iconic meeting spot for sailors and adventurers.

Day 8-9: São Jorge - The Vertical Island

Day 8:

- **Ferry to São Jorge.**
- **Check-in**: Cantinho das Buganvílias Resort.
- **Day-long hike**: Traverse the **Fajãs** of São Jorge, flat land areas at the base of cliffs where unique microclimates exist, and traditional agriculture flourishes.

Day 9:

- **Morning**: Coasteering along São Jorge's rugged coastline, combining swimming, climbing, and cliff jumping.
- **Afternoon**: Rest and relax at the hotel or explore the local area on your own.
- **Evening**: Dinner featuring São Jorge's famous cheese, a culinary adventure on its own.

Day 10-11: Return to São Miguel

Day 10:

- **Return to São Miguel.**
- **Afternoon**: Surfing lessons at **Ribeira Grande**'s beach, famous for its consistent waves.
- **Evening**: Explore more local dining options in Ponta Delgada.

Day 11:

- **Leisure day**: Optional activities based on interests, such as a repeat visit to a favorite spot or a relaxing day at the beach.
- **Final night**: Celebrate the adventure with a farewell dinner at **Restaurante Associação Agrícola de São Miguel**, known for its steaks and local cuisine.

Departure Day:

- **Departure from Ponta Delgada**, filled with thrilling memories of an action-packed visit to the Azores.

Conclusion

As we wrap up our exploration of the Azores, it's evident that these islands are more than just a scenic retreat. They embody a lifestyle deeply rooted in nature and heritage, with each island narrating its own unique story. From São Miguel's volcanic wonders to Terceira's historical alleys, from Pico's majestic heights to Faial's tranquil harbors, every corner of the Azores offers a distinct flavor of life.

Through this guide, we've journeyed together across these vibrant islands, uncovering the best experiences they have to offer—from soaking in hot springs under starlit skies to savoring the freshness of the Atlantic at our tables, and from heart-pumping adventures across rugged terrains to tranquil moments in hidden coves. We've revisited tales of ancient eruptions, navigators who charted unknown waters, and resilient communities that have thrived in this lush, oceanic wilderness.

This guide hopes to have shown that the Azores are not merely a destination but a living, pulsating experience—a rich blend of green islands, blue seas, and the vivid lives that flourish here.

For those poised to set foot in these islands, may this book serve as a beacon, guiding you to the heart of the Azores. For those who have traveled through these pages, may it be a gentle nudge to return and delve even deeper into the island life.

Embracing the Azores means embracing a world where nature, history, and culture harmonize effortlessly. Whether you carry these islands back home in your thoughts or linger here, letting the slow rhythm of island life color your days, keep the spirit of the Azores alive—a spirit defined by endurance, warmth, and the untamed beauty of the natural world.

Thank you for letting this guide accompany you on your Azorean adventure. May the memories of your travels inspire continuous discovery and bring you back to these islands, where the welcome is always warm, and the journey is forever new.

Safe travels!

Made in the USA
Coppell, TX
25 October 2024

39188783R00089